Living Jung

Marie-Louise von Franz, Honorary Patron

**Studies in Jungian Psychology
by Jungian Analysts**

Daryl Sharp, General Editor

Living Jung

The Good and the Better

Daryl Sharp

For all the ships at sea

Canadian Cataloguing in Publication Data

Sharp, Daryl, 1936-
    Living Jung: the good and the better

(Studies in Jungian psychology by Jungian analysts; 72)

Includes bibliographical references.

ISBN 0-919123-73-2

1. Jung, C.G. (Carl Gustav), 1875-1961.
2. Psychoanalysis. 3. Subconsciousness.
I. Title. II. Series.

BF173.S53 1996   150.19'54   C95-932810-6

INNER CITY BOOKS
Box 1271, Station Q, Toronto, Canada M4T 2P4
Telephone (416) 927-0355
FAX 416-924-1814

Honorary Patron: Marie-Louise von Franz.
Publisher and General Editor: Daryl Sharp.
Senior Editor: Victoria Cowan.

INNER CITY BOOKS was founded in 1980 to promote the
understanding and practical application of the work of C.G. Jung.

Cover: "Traversing the Void" (1986-90), wall piece by Jerry Pethick;
galvanized metal, enameled steel, mirror, glass, plywood,
aluminum frame, glass fluorescent tube. (Author's collection)

Index by the author

Printed and bound in Canada by
University of Toronto Press Incorporated

Contents

See final page for descriptions of other Inner City Books

Adam Brillig by Rachel

1
Mayday Malone's

The world turns, with us on it. We can only hope we don't fall off. Anything more is gravy. Like my getting together with Professor Adam Brillig, retired Jungian analyst and my sometime mentor.

"Living Young?" asked Adam on the phone. I had called him to arrange a meeting. "That's good! Oh, Living *Jung;* that's better. Say, would that mean live as if you were, or live up to? And if the latter, or indeed the former, would you have in mind something like the imitation of Christ?"

Adam Brillig is eighty-eight years old. His body is giving out, but his mind is still sharp. We had collaborated before, and now I had a new book in mind. Frankly, I wasn't at all sure I needed him for this one; his idiosyncratic bombast might well take over. On the other hand, I have a great respect for Adam, second only to my feeling for Jung. I don't always agree with them, but they make me think. I suppose I project onto them a wisdom they may or may not have. But does it matter either way? "A truth is a truth," said Jung, "when it works."[1] Of course that isn't necessarily so just because Jung said it, but it might be.

All I know for sure is that when I'm in a quandary I read Jung and if it persists I call Adam. And to tell the truth—well, mine—though I had a good idea of what I wanted to say, I had run dry on how to say it.

Adam had agreed to meet at 6:30 in his neighborhood pub, Mayday Malone's. Now there's a name to fire the imagination. I crossed the threshold with Sunny closely leashed,[2] thinking of the traditional cry for help from ships at sea ("M-a-y-d-a-y!") and then of Samuel Beckett's comic masterpiece, *Malone Dies.* Which is to say that for me Mayday Malone's conjured up echoes of the ultimate opposites, life and death.

It was not my first visit to Mayday's; more than once I had conferred

---

[1] "Some Crucial Points in Psychoanalysis," *Freud and Psychoanalysis,* CW 4, par. 578. [CW refers throughout to *The Collected Works of C.G. Jung]*
[2] Sunny is a Collie-Shepherd bitch of advanced age.

there with Adam in a back booth. But I lived some distance away and due to the press of business I was not a frequent patron. As a matter of fact I am not a frequent patron anywhere because in my life my house is where the action is. A small practice and a publishing business keep me hopping. Except for early morning jaunts to the post office to pick up what's in the box—and time spent with my artist friend Rachel and our daughter J.K., who have their own house—I leave home reluctantly.

On the whole, my daily mood depends on what I find in the box. A bunch of orders? Fan mail? A new foreign language edition? My heart sings. Empty? Bills? Advertising flyers? Another New Age journal soliciting ads? Blah. Worse than anything is the weekend because the post office is closed and there's no mail at all. Most people dread returning to work on Monday morning. Not me. And when I'm coming back from a week away my excitement reaches a fever pitch. I always look forward to what might be in the box. And there's never ever enough.

Now there's a paradox. I don't like going out, but my life revolves around what comes in from outside. Go figure. Typologically I think of myself as an introvert. I relate to the world subjectively, in terms of what's going on in me. I could be quite happy alone in a corner. But what to do, then, about my extraverted shadow? How would he survive? Franz Kafka, who incidentally professed a low opinion of psychology, nevertheless had an intuitive feel for the opposites; he wrote:

> Whoever leads a solitary life, and yet now and then wants to attach himself somewhere; whoever, according to changes in the time of day, the weather, the state of his business and the like, suddenly wishes to see any arm at all to which he might cling—he will not be able to manage for long without a window looking on to the street.[3]

Adam too is reclusive. In times past he sailed the seas, climbed mountains, went underground. He was a gourmet cook, active as an analyst and on the lecture circuit, a popular speaker on arcane subjects. That was years ago. Now he putters about in his laboratory on the top floor of an old Victorian mansion, and welcomes vistors who bring low-fat food.

Adam and I have two things in common; well, three. He too did his

---

[3] "The Street Window," in *The Penal Colony,* p. 39.

analytic training in Zürich, he is loath to leave home and he likes pubs. There is a notable fourth: his life has been informed for some forty years by Jung's ideas, as has my own for twenty-five. Not that we worship Jung. We're much too savvy for that. But if Jungian psychology ever became a religion—which I for one do not promote—we would probably qualify as high priests. Call us acolytes, fair enough.

On the other hand, Adam and I are also quite different. I am a classical linear thinker. I go from A to B to C, step by plodding step. Adam is given to formidable leaps of the imagination that leave me groping in the alphabet. He's a great talker; I like to listen. Adam is flamboyant in company, the center of attention; I prefer the back row. Physically, I am six feet of muscle, honed solid around a thousand pool tables. Adam is a four-and-a-half foot dwarf with a Buddha-belly who once skied down the Eiger.

I sidled into a corner booth to await the little man. Sunny sprawled at my feet.

Winona, young and pretty, ambled over balancing a tray.[4]

"Hi, haven't seen you lately," she smiled.

"Me either," I winked.

I ordered a pint of Algonquin, a natural draft brewed in a small Ontario border town. It has no chemicals except beer. Actually it doesn't taste all that different from the multinational brands, but it does feel greener.

Mayday Malone's is an English-style pub, and a sports bar. English pubs are all over the world now, designed to make you think you're just a few feet away from Trafalgar Square. In such places I have identified with the greats—Dante, Homer, Kafka, Dostoyevsky, Rilke, Kierkegaard and a dozen others. Although I've fallen out of love with England I still feel at home in a pub.

Mayday's was crowded this Friday night, a week before Christmas in the year of our Lord 1994. There were half a dozen television sets spotted around the room on shelves, broadcasting games from around the world. On two there was hockey; others featured golf, soccer, curling. Off to one

---

[4] Winona was not her real name; it was my friend Arnold's code-name for any woman he lusted for on sight.

side a group played darts. There was a bar billiards table, shuffleboard, pin-ball machines. People milled about, drinking, laughing, shouting. For a moment I imagined I was back in London, in Finches on the Fulham Road, young and fancy-free. But I no longer cared for the noise, nor did I wish to turn back the clock to when I did.

Watching the door I saw Adam sweep in. He climbed on a chair to hang cape, cane and beret on a hook by the door, then turned to survey the room. Over a sea of heads he spotted me. He hopped down and limped over, greeting other regulars on the way.

"Boyo-boyo!" he said, rubbing his hands briskly, for it was chilly out. Snow was falling and angels were in the wings. Near the bar there was a miniature tree, a real spruce, with colored balls and tinsel and lights that went on and off, perhaps in sync with music drowned out by the cacophonous blast from the TVs.

I raised my glass in greeting and bent forward to hear him. His eyes sparkled as he looked around.

"I love this place," he shouted. "In Mayday Malone's I have been elated, depressed and indifferent. In Mayday's by any name I have had some of my most significant thoughts. Of course I've also had many that were banal. Sorting wheat from chaff—isn't that what life's about?"

He said this airily, as if it had just occurred to him. Adam's like that. He seems to talk off the top of his head, but I suspect he seldom says anything he hasn't thought out.

He was wearing a black turtle-neck under a Tilley safari vest, tailor-made small, over khaki twill pants. I had on a white tee-shirt, gray cords and an off-the-rack Hugo Boss linen jacket, green, full of holes.[5]

Winona appeared. She and Adam seemed to have a special rapport. They tersely flirted.

"Hey you," she said.

Adam's eyes moved from hers to the tiny diamond in her belly-button, cheerfully exposed between tank-top and tight cut-off jeans. He looked up at her and wrinkled his nose.

---

[5] I have always found it hard to discard worn-out things—clothes, books, cars, lovers. I become attached, like they were pieces of my soul. That's called projection. I know better, but there you are.

She tossed her head. "Half a Guinness, old guy?"

"Make it a big one," said Adam, "why not."

Winona turned to me. "Another for you?"

"Please," I said, "and Scotch on the rocks. Glenmorangie?"

She nodded. "We have all the single malts."

Adam watched her as she moved off.

"An interesting young lady," he said, "self-confident, provocative, on the brink of life. She works here nights while she studies archaeology. Oh yes, she's not thick, you know. A trifle naive, perhaps, but who is not at her age?"

A rhetorical question I could not gainsay anyway.

"I wonder what goes on in her head," mused Adam. "I'd never ask, of course, but I do wonder. What are her fantasies? Do you suppose she thinks of that gem in her navel as just a fashionable ornament? Eh? Or does she see it as I do, metaphorically, as the tip of her inner treasure hard to attain? Hmm? What do you think?"

I said nothing. I used to have a ready response to just about anything. I was chock-full of opinions. Never mind where they came from, where they went or what they were worth. Now before speaking I reflect on what I really think and feel. I consider who's listening and the circumstances. This can become uncomfortable in a group, especially when the talk turns to issues about which I know enough to be ambivalent. Silence is seldom received as golden. Eyebrows are raised, fingers tapped, sometimes tempers rise. Without an opinion, who are you? What do you stand for? What's your bottom line? Fair questions, but how to speak and what to say when tongue is tied considering context, complex and archetype— that sort of thing? The unreflective are socially more acceptable. They speak their complexes and just about nobody notices.

Once in a while I find myself with someone who isn't desperate for an answer. One such is Rachel, who doesn't need me to validate her, and another is this old gaffer who can barely walk. Oh, Adam does run on at times, but he is not unreflective.

"I am reminded of my rake-hell days," he was saying. "I was a puer with a vengeance. Oh my, I was. You know of my years in a monastery. When I got out I was at pains to make up for lost time. Phallos ruled. I courted both sexes, but at heart I was a ladies' man. They patted my head and fell at my feet. I was Don Juan incarnate, like Krishna with his bevy of milk-maids. Remember that song by Janis Joplin—'Get It While You Can'? Well I did my best.

"Of course that was in the good old days, when one didn't fear being struck down by some venereal scourge or a killer like AIDS. Never mind that I risked my life in other ways—on mountains, in caves and jungles and night clubs. I was young; death by any means had no dominion."

Adam prattled on about his dissolute life as if he were speaking to himself. I didn't mind because I fancied that one day, in answer to a clamoring demand, I would be called upon to tell his story from beginning to end.

"When I was forty-four," he said, "I suddenly found myself impotent. This was bad enough in the boudoir, but in my business life—which at that time involved brokering medical supplies to Third World countries—it was devastating. You see, my lack of phallic thrust was not only physical. Where I had been a man who knew his mind and spoke it, I became uncertain, indecisive, tentative. I doubted everything, and most of all myself. For some time I faced the day with a brave front, or just stayed in bed, but in the end I sought professional help.

"First I went to a psychiatrist. He listened to my story and smiled. 'You are suffering from a chemical imbalance.' He gave me an assortment of pills. 'Take a red when you get up and one before going to bed. The yellows are for feeling glum in-between. Take a green if you feel suicidal, but do call my secretary before you take a purple. Good luck.'

"I took the reds and yellows and felt worse. I took a green and still felt like throwing myself off a cliff. So I consulted a Freudian anlayst.

" 'I can help,' she said. She was beautiful, her office was not; cold steel, impersonal. 'It will take time of course . . . childhood traumas, erotic conflicts, so on and so forth. I shall need to see you four times a week for at least five years. I trust you are a man of means.'

"The Adlerian I went to was blunt. 'You are small, you would like to be big. You have unconsciously arranged your life to have power over others. Be honest now, aren't some of your best friends tall?'

"At my wit's end I saw a Jungian. He heard me out and shrugged. "I don't know what your problem is," he said, "but I believe you do. No one can find a cure for it but you; no one but you can identify it as a cure. And once you find it, no one but you can do anything about it. Do you dream?'

"I worked with him once a week for the next three years. Then I found my way to Zürich."

Adam settled back and stroked his goatee. He adjusted his glasses; the lenses were as thick as the bottom of a bottle. He looked me up and down, noting my tattered threads.

"Well, young fellow," he said, "what's on your mind?"

You would think I'd be grateful for the opening, having called on him for just this. But in fact his condescending manner irked me. It's true that I am young relative to him, but I'm glad to be quit of youth. I am a Capricorn, an astrological sign under which those who are born are said to age well and eagerly. I can believe it. I am sixty; I treasure my spare tire and I don't miss my hair. I look forward to being a senior citizen.

Across from Adam in Mayday's, my mind shuffled through some possible retorts. I could point out that without me he did not exist. I swallowed that because it was just as likely that I did not exist without him. I toyed briefly with the notion that Adam and I, despite the age difference, were peers. I could not sustain this. Then I thought of times my father put me down. When I was twelve I had a job after school selling eggs door to door. One day I dropped a carton and was fired. "You can't do anything right," said my dad. When I didn't make the high-school baseball team he said, "You are a great disappointment to me." When I was twenty-two and defected from Procter & Gamble he said I'd always regret it.

"Take your time," drawled Adam. He pulled out his pipe and turned his attention to the milling crowd.

Well, shoot. Adam was not my father and I was a grown man. I had made my way in the world and now I was a man of substance, answerable to no one. Why, then, did I suddenly feel like a kid?

Clearly I was complexed.

Now isn't that typical. Just when you think you're in charge, you're reminded again that you're not. There are those who say you can overcome your complexes, but the best I've been able to do is to identify a few and know when they're active. Nor does that always stop me from acting them out.

I pulled myself together and addressed Adam as follows.

"From the many communications I have received of late, it appears that interest among the educated lay public in the problems of the human psyche is becoming more serious. New Age pursuits are on the wane. Channeling and crystals, auras, pendulums, past lives and the like have not delivered the goods. People are waking up to their same old neurotic selves. I believe they are now more open than ever to Jung's views on the nature and influence of the unconscious. Why 'Living Jung'? Well, because to me, and in my life, Jung's ideas are not dead dogma."

This was rather more than I usually say out loud at any one time. I stopped for breath.

Adam said nothing. His eyes bored into mine, seeking—it seemed to me—my real motive. Fame? Fortune? Posterity? Nothing else to do? I shrank before his penetrating look, for I could not deny any of it. Whatever I might say, the opposite was there too. My only defense would be that while feathering my own nest I might incidentally do some broader good. Feeble, perhaps, but close to my truth.

"You understand it is not a question of imitating Jung's actual life," I added, having in mind Adam's query on the phone, "but rather how one might conduct oneself in light of his momentous discoveries."

The TVs blared. Someone scored on one and the din increased. Several burly young fellows linked arms and danced. Girls jumped up and did the same. Adam laughed and clapped and swayed to the music. It was infectious and I joined in. Sunny covered her ears.

It was all over in a few minutes. Adam turned to me.

"That's chaff for you," he said, "and there's a good deal to be said for it, at least when you're young. Let the spirit flow! Without chaff, would there be wheat? Jung himself was none too conscious in his early years, as you know. And who is? We laugh and sing, cry and grumble; one way or another we get through the day. And what's wrong with that? Good luck, I say. Until you're on your knees there's no need to question the front of your face.

"Ah, but what then, when the old ways no longer work? What do you do about the goblins? When Jung came to that point he went inside and discovered his parts unknown. And from his experience came a model of the psyche that is of inestimable value to everyone."

This was exactly what I wanted to hear.

"Personally," said Adam, "I regard the existence of the unconscious as a fact so important and so topical that in my opinion it would be a great loss if its manifestations were to be found only in technical journals gathering dust in libraries. If ever there was a time when self-knowledge was the absolutely necessary and right thing, it is now. People are hungry for substance. They have no end of cake, but long for bread.

"Jung tells of an old peasant woman who wrote asking if she might see him just once. He invited her to come. She was very poor—intellectually too. She had not even finished primary school. She kept house for her brother; they ran a little newsstand. Jung asked her if she really understood his books which she said she had read. And she replied, 'Your books are not books, Herr Professor, they are bread.' "6

Adam became thoughtful. I shut the outside off and focused on a tiny mole just above his left eyebrow.

"The world is in a God-awful mess," he said. "We are living in a time of great disruption. Political passions are aflame, internal upheavals have brought nations to the brink of chaos. So what else is new? The psychology of the individual is reflected in the psychology of the nation. Only a change in the attitude of individuals can initiate a change in the psychology of the nation.

"One of the great problems in our culture is that extraversion is overvalued. Introversion is generally viewed as a somewhat shady activity, if not downright selfish. Being active in the world is deemed to be the measure of one's worth. You don't become Citizen of the Year on account of the time you spend staring at the wall, and you don't get the Order of Merit for working on your dreams. Yet collective change involves first of all a change in oneself, which in turn requires an introspective system of accounting. And whoever gives careful consideration to personal life-

---

6 *C.G. Jung Speaking: Interviews and Encounters,* p. 416. Adam did not, of course, footnote his conversation. To assist the reader I have sought out his references and give them when possible.

events is bound to come up against the frontiers of the unconscious, which contains precisely what they need—bread, so to speak."

"You are on-side, then?" I whispered. Something was caught in my throat.

"On-side!?" cried Adam. "Yes!—on-side and back-side too!"

His hands flew out and knocked over my pint. Beer flowed into my lap; the glass smashed on the floor.

Winona waltzed over.

"What's up, gents?"

"Dear girl, I was making a point," said Adam, looking sheepish. "Pray, bring a dustpan."

I dabbed napkins on my pants and shoes. Adam looked around and knit his brow.

"Mayday Malone's is close to my heart," he said. "It is a fine venue for fun and games, for fellowship, for sorting yourself out. But tonight there is too much noise. Everyone agrees that noise is one of the evils of our time, but would we have it if we didn't secretly want it? There is a widespread though not generally conscious fear that loves noise because it stops the fear from being heard; it drowns out the instinctive inner warnings. This kind of fear seeks noisy company to scare away the demons. People alone and in silence might reflect, and there's no knowing what might then come up."

He stood up. "Let us debouche to my place. Do you agree? Fine! Pick up the tab, would you? There's a good fellow."

2
Jung and Restless

"Some thirty years ago," said Adam, "I was sojourning in the Himalayas when a group of local women organized a protest movement against the desecration of their environment by Big Business. Among other things, they adopted the tactic of embracing trees in order to protect them against commercial logging. The government sided with the loggers."

My eyes wandered as Adam talked. His place consisted of several attic rooms with the walls knocked out to make a long low studio, ventilated by a huge window at one end. Under the window—which incidentally had an excellent view of the street—was piled up the usual apparatus of a physico-chemical laboratory: flasks and retorts, Bunsen burners, jars, bottles and packets. We were stretched out on soft rugs and leather cushions, which made the low-ceilinged room seem more spacious.

The weather had turned foul. Sleet and snow beat the windows and thunder rolled. Sunny looked anxious and huddled as close to me as she could get.

"Troops were sent in," said Adam, "authorized to shoot anyone who stood in their way. But this didn't work. Perhaps the men decided that shooting a woman in the act of hugging a tree might not play too well on the evening news. Thinking they might have more success with dumb animals, the government and loggers sent in elephants to trample the women. Being obedient army elephants, they moved in on command."

Through Adam's studio wound a pebble path bordered by shrubs and bushes in pots and crates—cactus plants, small conifers, dwarf palms and rhododendrons. Along the path, hung on the bushes or dangling from the ceiling, were dozens of little placards and photographs, each one carrying a drawing or an inscription. Against the walls were terrariums and cages holding various fauna: spiders, termites, white mice, ant-eaters, axolotls. Interspersed were magazines and papers and journals, and books, books, books. I had been to Adam's many times, but I was still bemused by his living space. "A cornucopian delight," he once called it. To me, fastidiously tidy, it was simply disarray.

17

"As you know," continued Adam, "the god Ganesha in the Hindu pantheon is worshipped in the form of an elephant. There is an annual festival for this god, during which Hindu women sing a ritual song and bedeck the temple elephants with colored ribbons and garlands of flowers.

"Now, as the army elephants approached, the women left the trees, moving forward and singing until they eventually swarmed over the animals, stroking them and embracing their massive trunks and feet. The elephants responded by kneeling and could not be induced to rise. Troops and loggers withdrew. The government subsequently fell, replaced by authorities who passed new laws protecting trees.

"What can we learn from this incident? That elephants have a soft spot for women? That temple elephants can somehow communicate with their conscripted military brethren? That women are brave? Certainly it took courage to peel themselves away from the trees and face an unpredictable phalanx of behemoths. Maybe such acts capture our imagination because they are a spontaneous and spectacular expression of the more patient, enduring kind of heroism exemplified by females for hundreds and thousands of years. For what do such women personify if not a dazzling commitment to embrace life in whatever form—husband, baby, tree or elephant? What do you think, eh?"

I refilled our glasses from the bottle of Beaujolais-Villages Adam had placed between us.

"The other day," I said, "I received an artist's sketch of a turtle flying out of the eye of an elephant. Isn't that an intriguing image?" Second only, I was thinking, to a dream I once had of a spider on skis, riding a razor blade. Who says the unconscious has no sense of humor?

"Perhaps," I ventured, "those Himalayan women sang to the elephants in a pure act of faith."

Adam nodded. "I believe you have struck the nail on its head. The fruits of what we call the Age of Enlightenment—science, reason and logic—are ubiquitous but not all-inclusive. There have always been those who would die for a principle, against all reason and sanity. There will always be some among us who will walk toward elephants, singing hymns of praise, without regard for their personal safety. There will always be those who will embrace trees and the rough, huge feet sent to crush them. Many will indeed be crushed, for that is the way of the world. But sometimes the beasts will kneel and pray along with them, a prayer of peace and harmony. Those elephants and those women praying together may be the clearest manifestation of God that humankind has ever seen."

Sunny stirred and licked my foot. I rubbed her snout.

"It may be," said Adam, "that such foolish, brave singers are humanity's salvation. Some embracers of trees and huggers of elephants may even become pregnant, in time giving birth to themselves."

I thought this pretty unlikely, but as usual when I was with Adam I was willing to suspend disbelief. More, had I not run afoul of my own rational mind? Had I not put my faith in Logos and pooh-poohed my personal feelings? Had my reasoned view of what was right and proper not brought me to my knees? Dostoyevsky's Underground Man said:

> Reason is a good thing. No argument about that. But reason is only reason, and it only satisfies man's rational requirements. Desire, on the other hand, is the manifestation of life . . . . And although, when we're guided by our desires, life may often turn into a messy affair, it's still life and not a series of extractions of square roots.[7]

"I recently had occasion to look up some of the references to elephants in Jung's Collected Works," continued Adam. "A most interesting lot! As far back as 1912, in a lecture given at Fordham University in New York, Jung referred to elephants in speaking about the hypothesis that associations to the images in dreams can lead to a clearer understanding of the dream's message. He spoke of a man who scoffed that by means of psychoanalytic interpretations one could even connect a cucumber with an elephant! Jung said:

> This worthy showed us, by the very fact of associating "cucumber" with "elephant," that the two things somehow have an associative connection in his mind. One must have a lot of nerve and a magisterial judgment to declare that the human mind produces entirely meaningless associations. In this instance, only a little reflection is needed to understand the meaning of the association.[8]

---

[7] *Notes from Underground,* pp. 105-106.

[8] "The Theory of Psychoanalysis," *Freud and Psychoanalysis,* CW 4, par. 337.

I must say this baffled me—I, an aficionado of elephants, and also, by the way, of cucumbers—but I said nothing.

"In a later treatise," Adam went on, "Jung referred to Pliny's description of the fabled unicorn as having a horse's body, an elephant's feet and the tail of a wild boar.[9] He quoted tales of Queen Maya's conception of the Buddha through the penetration of her side by a white elephant's trunk, contrasting this with the medieval tradition of Mary's conception of Jesus through the ear.[10] And he noted that the elephant is only one among many theriomorphic symbols of the Self that turn up in dreams, along with lions, snakes, dragons, bears and other powerful beasts."[11]

Adam disappeared then. I was glad to be spared a response for I was full up to here with elephants.

I stared at one thing and another. Disarray or delight, the surroundings were conducive to meditation. A hanging postcard near me showed a bespectacled gentleman behind whom a laughing lady swung naked from a chandelier. The caption read: **Jung and Restless.** Beside that were photographs of Adam—on a beach holding an iguana; on roller skates; in climbing gear; hugging a lovely on a cruise ship; pensive in a book-lined study. Another card pictured an old man tottering about in a walker behind a flapping chicken who cried, "This guy is falling! This guy is falling!" The caption: **Shattering the Myth of Chicken Little.** A variety of plants hung from hooks in the ceiling. The walls were crowded with prints and paintings, among which were two by Rachel: a sketch of Adam in his birthday suit and a charcoal study of a nude female torso.

There was nothing in sight that didn't put me into a spin.

I listened to Adam bustling about in his kitchenette, a screened-off corner at one end. I thought of what he'd said about himself in Mayday's. Adam Brillig as puer; it was hard to imagine.

"Adam," I called, "that puer business in your early life, what was that all about?"

---

[9] "Alchemical Symbolism in the History of Religion," *Psychology and Alchemy,* CW 12, par. 526n.
[10] *Symbols of Transformation,* CW 5, par. 490.
[11] See "The Psychological Aspects of the Kore," *The Archetypes and the Collective Unconscious,* CW 9i, par. 315; also *Aion,* CW 9ii, par. 356.

"Eh?" he called back.

Two minutes later he emerged with a steaming tray of crisp bacon and pancakes—better say crêpes, they were so thin—with black Swedish caviar *(svart stenbitsrom)* on the side, no less.

"My friend," he said. "You come too seldom. Let us celebrate. Damn the cholesterol! And a new book in the making! Now that's something; it was such fun last time. How is the winsome Rachel, anyway? What a delicate touch with a brush. And J.K.? Now there's a lass with a future. Here, help yourself to rolls and huckleberry jam, and this is real maple syrup from Quebec, not that yuk made from corn-cobs."

We clinked glasses and dug in. I was hungrier than I knew. As we ate I brought Adam up to date on the doings of Rachel and J.K. Then for a few minutes we sat comfortably in silence. I slipped some juicy scraps to Sunny. She'd had her measure of meal before Mayday's but she forever hankers for a snack.

"Adam," I said finally, "that puer business . . . ?"

"I did hear you," said Adam. "I've been thinking."

He took our empty plates to the sink and came back with a bottle of three-star Napoleon brandy. He settled on a cushion and tamped his pipe. I rolled a cigarette. A cuckoo clock struck eleven, way past Sunny's bedtime, and mine too. She was still alert, sniffing around the cages. I could feel myself beginning to fade, but Adam was not.

"Picture this," he said. "I was a middle-aged man but I behaved like an adolescent. As a matter of fact I was a textbook puer. I looked younger than my age and was proud of it; I was driven by my instincts and gave little thought to the effect my actions had on others; I acted spontaneously, prone to do what felt right, though what felt right one minute often felt wrong the next. I bent every effort to please others, and in return I expected from them the love and affection I'd had from my mother as a child—just for being who I was. In short, I moved through life irresponsibly, without having grown up.

"For many years this worked. I was not unhappy. Oh, some desires were thwarted, but I blamed others for that. Troubling dreams were easily dismissed in the light of day. I was active in the world, master of my destiny. I had no knowledge of an inner life, and felt no need of one. I dare say I would have continued in this way indefinitely had something in me not rebelled. Only then, as I said earlier, was I forced to seek counsel."

I was wide awake now and avid for more.

"As an analyst I worked with many puers," said Adam. "Invariably they were under the spell of a positive mother complex, as I had been.

"I remember one man close to forty who owned a small antique business. He was not married but he was close to many women. He was idealistic, trusting everyone, always in debt. He had a litany of complaints, both physical and emotional—upset stomach, heartburn, bad moods, depression, conflict and so on. I read these symptoms as an attempt at self-cure: his attitude was wrong; he was ill adapted both to the reality of his outer life and to the reality of himself.

"After some months he dreamt of a huge green woman with great hanging breasts. She was terrifying and he ran from her. He woke up crying. He had no personal associations, so I called his attention to the classic Indian goddess Kali, known as the giver of life who may instead deliver death—one among countless mythological images of the opposites in the guise of the Great Mother."

"Kali," I said. "Isn't she often pictured with multiple boobs?"

"No, that's Diana of Ephesus, but the same principle applies: a breast may hold not milk but poison. After this man had done some research, I encouraged him to confront Madame Green, as we called her, in active imagination. You know, play pretend, like when you were very young and sang to flowers; there were ghosts under the bed and trees talked back. Our early ancestors lived that life; reality as they knew it. Animism, we call it now, though we still knock on wood.

"Anyway, he did so. He approached her in a little boat, but she just laughed and shooed him away. We surmised that she had something to do with his mother complex and his romantic view of life. But what exactly? What was the unconscious trying to tell him? And what could he do with the information? Then in outer life he became obsessed with a somewhat hysterical woman—a girl, rather, barely half his age—who behaved just as a nature demon would. She teased and provoked but could not be pinned down.

"So here he had the Great Mother in his dreams, too scary to be accessible, and synchronistically a skittish real-life personification of that arche-type. Now he was up against it. He could see a connection but he couldn't do anything about it. He acknowledged that his inflamed desire for the girl was conceivably due to the projection of something in him— and I can tell you, even that much took more than a few weeks—but all the same he still felt helpless.

"I suggested that he talk to this girl in himself as if she were real. Again, pretend but in earnest. When he did so she said, 'I am the same as the green lady with whom you could not talk,' implying that she was immortal, like the archetype. He said he couldn't accept that, and she answered that she was the beginning and the end—meaning she was God! Well, that shook him up. He was a lapsed Catholic and for some time he thought seriously of renewing his faith. Then a long conversation started in which his whole Weltanschauung had to be reevaluated. Over the next few months he had to review and reconsider every aspect of his life and attitudes, as she pulled them to pieces bit by bit.

"That's how it goes when you work on yourself. Through a personal complex you become acquainted with the archetype. In this case, the green woman, on the archetypal level, was practically unapproachable. The next step mythologically is Kore-Persephone, the mother goddess in a younger form; he could speak to her. You see, the daughter goddess is closer to the human than the mother, just as God the father is more removed from humanity than Christ the son.

"So it seemed to me that what was going on in this man's psyche could be viewed in terms of the Demeter-Persephone myth. When the carefree Persephone was snatched underground by Hades, her mother Demeter roamed the world in mourning. Similarly, a man confronted with the loss of his youth may be bereft. His task then is to get to know his anima—the archetype of life. That's not news to you, I'm sure. What do you think?"

It was a lot to digest. I played for time.

"What happened to the real woman, the girl?" I asked.

"Oh, he lost interest in her soon enough. Mind you, that wasn't inevitable. Initially she was a magnet for his complex. He could have any woman he wanted—except this one. That was certainly part of the hook.

More important, I think, was that she was as undeveloped emotionally as his own inner woman. Once he had a handle on his psychology the girl lost her numinosity and he saw her more as she really was—a rather simple-minded coquette who wasn't even particularly attractive."

"Good thing he didn't marry her!" I said.

Adam nodded. "Of course many do marry the one who hooks them, and it isn't always a mistake. It depends on what happens when the projection falls away, when the person you fell in love with turns out to be somebody else—like as not, yourself.[12] Instinct drives us to couple; relationship is something else. Coupling is good, relationship can be better,.

"In any case, this man I speak of did not have marriage on his mind. Far from it. He made that very clear to women before he had his way with them—or they with him. As if in this way he escaped responsibility for what he did. 'I don't fall in love,' he said to me once. 'I make it, beautifully. I shine my little light into any dark hole, and many a bleak life glows briefly.'

"His problem, you see, besides inflation, was Don Juanism, which contrary to the popular image of the type has very little to do with conquest. More often it is rooted in the desire to give pleasure and gain approval; that is one of the many consequences of the positive mother complex, and promiscuity is by no means its only expression.

"Naturally he was not aware of this. Consciously he only knew he was attracted to women, and they to him, and he could think of no reason to say No. I did not presume to judge his behavior. But clearly his symptoms—including occasional impotence—indicated an unconscious need to establish a relationship with the anima, which would mean incarnating the archetype of the feminine. The green goddess in this man's dream was completely maternal, and the hysterical outer woman was the anima in classical form. She had certain characteristics that represented his specific anima, who would in time manifest as his emotional and feeling

---

[12] Jung: "Just as we tend to assume that the world is as we see it, we naively suppose that people are as we imagine them to be. . . . projecting our own psychology into our fellow human beings. . . . All human relationships swarm with these projections." ("General Aspects of Dream Psychology," *The Structure and Dynamics of the Psyche,* CW 8, par. 507)

life. But first he had to meet her outside, as we all do. That is seen in one way as the incarnation of the goddess, and in another as the long, slow process of individuation.

"There is nothing abnormal about a romantic attitude when one is young. Only later in life, when you've had some disappointing experiences, do you come up against the cynical, realistic side of relationship. A degree of cynicism about love is healthy and necessary. No grown-up person can be only romantic. That goes against nature, and so does an endless succession of superficial relationships. This man had tried to ignore his internal unease but his own psyche would not let him. Frankly it was not a difficult case, since I had been through something similar myself. Otherwise I would have had only theory to go on, and that is a poor substitute for experience."

Sunny snored softly. I cast my mind back.

"When I was training in Zürich," I said, "there was a lot of talk among the students about puer psychology. Von Franz's book, *The Problem of the Puer Aeternus,* had recently been published. I did not discuss it with a single man who didn't feel he fit the profile—more or less of a mother's boy, idealistic, somewhat effeminate, artistically inclined, fantasies of grandeur and so on. Even most of the women readily confessed to being puellas, meaning they recognized the puer aspect of their animus."

Adam nodded.

"Ovid speaks of the god Eros as the original *puer aeternus,* the eternal child," he said. "That might be all right for gods, but it does not work for humans. In reality, the puer is a parasite on the mother, a creature of her imagination, who only lives when rooted in the maternal body. In actual psychic experience the mother corresponds to the collective unconscious, and the son to consciousness, which fancies itself free but must ever again succumb to the power of sleep and deadening unconsciousness.

"If a man lives as though he were eternal, as if he didn't need to adapt to reality and a real woman, if he lives in fantasies of one day saving the world or being the greatest philosopher or writer, he is identifying with the god Eros. His personal heroes are people like Cyrano de Bergerac and Don Quixote and others who tilt at windmills. His ego complex is stuck in the archetype and the collective scheme fits virtually all cases."

"Including mine," I admitted, flooded by memories.

"When I was in Zürich," said Adam, "I did some control work with von Franz."

"You didn't!" I was grabbed by envy.

"Indeed, and quite an experience it was. She lived in this little house in Küsnacht with the aging Barbara Hannah, a queen in her own right. It was late spring; we sat in the garden among growing things, or rather I did; von Franz would be on her knees with a trowel, planting or weeding. From time to time she lifted her head to comment on the case I presented. She had an uncanny knack for seeing archetypal patterns in what was going on in a person's everyday life. Her remarks were earthy and to the point; her mind was quick and she laughed a lot. I would have to say I picked up as much from her as I have from Jung.

"Anyway, she told me that when she first lectured on the puer aeternus, many people came up to her after and said they knew exactly who she was talking about, each one giving a different name! In fact, she said, she had spoken about a man who had never even been to Zürich; it was just that the characteristics she described fit so many cases.

"You see, there's nothing individual about someone who identifies with a god. They are enslaved by an archetype. If they pay attention when their psyche kicks up a fuss, there is the possibility of change. More often, I'm afraid, they dismiss their symptoms as due to something they ate, or blame their moods on someone else. If they remain unconscious they languish on the margin of life, forever at odds with family and friends, touchy, resentful, day-dreaming of better days to come."

I thought of my cranky old aunt in Saskatchewan. There she was in the middle of the prairie, a thousand miles from any sea. "One day my ship will come in," she'd say, scouring the horizon.

Sunny rose and shook herself, adding some fleas to Adam's collection of fauna. She faced me with ears erect. I stroked her sides and remembered that tomorrow I was to take her to the vet for her semiannual grooming and shots. I divided the remaining drops of brandy between Adam's glass and mine.

"I must go soon," I yawned.

"You are welcome to stay over," said Adam. "You and Sunny can have the honeymoon suite." He gestured to a cot in the corner.

I waved vaguely.

"Adam," I said, "what archetypal pattern do you think the puer is caught in?"

He stood up.

"Forgive me," he said. "My brain cells have shut down. Tomorrow afternoon I have an appointment with some TV nabobs who believe I have answers to the mystery of life. I think they might better bark up their own tree, but I'm vain enough not to want to disappoint them. Perhaps we can go on in the morning."

I felt in no condition to drive, so I accepted Adam's offer of a pillow and a moth-eaten sleeping bag.

"It's seen better days," he said apologetically, "but it kept me alive on Mount St. Helens. The thermal lining is good to about forty below. Sleep tight. I have first dibbs on the bathroom."

I trekked downstairs with Sunny and directed her to pee in a patch of grass. She did. On the way up her legs gave out. It wasn't the first time. She was fourteen, after all, old for dog-age. She sprawled between steps and looked at me dolefully.

"Good girl," I said, stroking her. "It's okay."

Together we stumbled back to Adam's where Sunny found a rug to scrunch up. I gave her a cookie from the supply I carry and instructed her to stay put. She didn't; I did.

3
The Good and the Better

There were two soft-boiled eggs and whole-wheat toast waiting for me when I got up at 6:30. I had dreamed of riding bare-back on a horse, galloping madly through dense forests and fields of hay. I awoke exhausted, wondering if maybe, just maybe, on some level we actually do live out the fantastical happenings in dreams. That would explain why we wake up tired when we dream of flying, say, or climbing a mountain.

This sounds more like a New Age fantasy then orthodox Jungian thinking. Still, it is reported that in von Franz's first meeting with Jung he told her of a woman who dreamed she was on the moon. Von Franz said, dismissively, "But that was a dream." Jung replied, "Oh, she *was* on the moon."[13] Maybe that was von Franz's first lesson in the reality of the unconscious.

According to Jung, all dream images are essentially subjective. He suggests thinking of a dream as if it were a theater in which the dreamer is at once the scene, the player, the prompter, the producer, the author, the public and the critic. Thus all the figures in dreams are personified aspects of the dreamer's own personality.[14] This means that when I dream of Miss X or Mr. Y, the unconscious is presenting me with information to add to the inventory of my self-image. What is there about me that is like him or her? In what ways do we differ? How do I feel about them? How does their appearance in the context of the dream reflect what is currently happening in my life?

And my dream horse? A bundle of instinctive energy on the loose, perhaps. But why a horse and not, say, a fox or a weasel or . . . an elephant? And to what end? And my associations to hay and forests?

As a kid I used to play in a hayloft on my uncle's farm, with my

---

[13] See Gilda Frantz, "I'll See You in My Dreams," in *Psychological Perspectives,* no. 31 (Spring-Summer 1995), p. 22.

[14] "General Aspects of Dream Psychology," *The Structure and Dynamics of the Psyche,* CW 8, par. 509.

cousin Jane. My first sexual experience, at age six, was tickling her private parts with a straw; my second, age seven, was her tickling mine. Then there's the parable of Buridan's ass, who starved to death between two piles of hay because he couldn't make a choice. Jung's comment on this, as an image of a conflict situation, was that the important thing was not whether the bundle on the right or the one on the left was the better, or which one he ought to eat first, but what he wanted in the depths of his being—which did he feel pushed toward?[15]

Very well, how might that apply to me?

Sunny interrupted my reveries with insistent demands of her own. I did not begrudge them; I think too much anyway.

Adam was bright and perky.

"I was up with the birds," he said as we ate. "I've been reading von Franz." He held up her book on Apuleius's classic, *The Golden Ass*. "Listen to this":

> The positive mother complex constellates the divine son-lover of the great goddess, and together they play the role of goddess and god, as Dr. Jung describes it in the first chapter of *Aion*. For a young man it is a great temptation to stay with the eternal mother, and he joins in by being the eternal lover. They cheat each other out of life and do not face the fact that they are ordinary human beings. The son cannot get away from the mother, and prefers to live the myth and the role of the eternal god.[16]

"That is the archetypal pattern the puer lives out," said Adam. "He is stuck in the paradise of the mother-world. He finds it difficult to adapt to life as he finds it, which is rather harsher than the maternal tit of plenty."

"That's your considered opinion?" I asked.

"That is my experience," said Adam.

Sunny gave Adam a lick. He fed her a crust.

"Von Franz refers to *Aion*," said Adam, "where Jung speaks of the secret conspiracy between mother and son, and how each helps the other to betray life. Remember?"

I was fuzzy. Adam dug it out:

---

[15] "The Structure of the Unconscious," *Two Essays*, CW 7, par. 487.
[16] *A Psychological Interpretation of the Golden Ass of Apuleius*, p. 70.

Where does the guilt lie? With the mother, or with the son? Probably with both. The unsatisfied longing of the son for life and the world ought to be taken seriously. There is in him a desire to touch reality, to embrace the earth and fructify the field of the world. But he makes no more than a series of fitful starts, for his initiative as well as his staying power are crippled by the secret memory that the world and happiness may be had as a gift—from the mother. The fragment of world which he, like every man, must encounter again and again is never quite the right one, since it does not fall into his lap, does not meet him half way, but remains resistant, has to be conquered, and submits only to force. It makes demands on the masculinity of a man, on his ardour, above all on his courage and resolution when it comes to throwing his whole being into the scales. For this he would need a faithless Eros, one capable of forgetting his mother and relinquishing the first love of his life.[17]

"That's a pretty powerful rant," I observed. It rang uncomfortably true.

"It's not all bad news," said Adam. "A man like that generally has a zest for life and is spurred to creative efforts beyond the ordinary. He deals with problems in a fresh and original way. He's always into something new, surrounded by a mysterious nimbus of vitality that is particularly appealing to those who live a hum-drum life. Primitives would describe him as having *mana,* a magical quality ascribed to gods and sacred objects. We sophisticates call it charisma. Unwittingly, just by being himself, the puer snares the unrequited. If he's the Don Juan type, he has his pick of women—or men, if he's gay. He makes an excellent con man too, because he genuinely believes in his incredible schemes.

"Of course a degree of the puer's vitality is necessary, otherwise one is old before one's time. But identification with the puer leads to the neurosis of the provisional life. One day, some day, the boy is going to be a great man. One's current lot is not what one really wants; one is always 'about to' take the step into real life. Some day one will do what is necessary—only not yet. As an aspect of the Self, the puer conveys the feeling of eternal life, of life beyond death. But the man who identifies with the

---

17 "The Syzygy: Anima and Animus," *Aion,* CW 9ii, par. 22. Von Franz explains "a faithless Eros" as "the capacity to turn away from time to time from a relationship . . . . The *puer aeternus,* in the negative sense of the word, very often tends to be too impressed, too weak, and too much of a 'good boy' in his relationships, without a quick self-defense reaction where required." (*Puer Aeternus,* p. 47)

puer lives in the wrong kind of eternity, an ethereal space with very thin air. He misses the here and now, the blood and guts of life on earth; that has to be accepted because it is what makes the bridge to eternal life.

"Von Franz writes that the picture is the reverse for the man with a negative mother complex":

> In the positive mother complex, the young man identifies with the puer aeternus and thus has to dis-identify . . . . In the case of the negative mother complex, the man dis-identifies too completely from the puer aeternus quality. But actually he seeks this quality of creativeness in himself, that is, he seeks what he lacks in himself. [He] tends to be cynical and not to trust his feeling, or women. He is in a state of constant restraint. He cannot give himself to life, but always seeks the "snake in the grass." . . . [So] the puer aeternus becomes a very important inner figure which has to be assimilated in order to progress from psychic miserliness and to counterbalance his frozen attitude to life.[18]

"That's the nub of it," said Adam. "The man with the positive mother complex, in his conscious behavior, takes great pains to please and tends to trust women rather too much. The one with a negative mother complex is overtly distrustful and possessive. But if you get to know them intimately, beneath the surface of the former you discover a jealous side, and behind the latter's wary front—a protective defense—there is a naive trusting shadow. They are brothers under the skin. That's consistent with Jung's model of the psyche, whereby the opposite of what one consciously is—our attitudes and feelings, the way we function and so on—also exists in oneself, but below the surface, so to speak."

The opposites again. I have experienced them often enough—in love-hate relationships, ambivalence, conflict and so on—but I still feel like a dummling. Theoretically, the archetypes are neutral containers of the opposites. For instance, the mother archetype is a primordial, instinctual image of "mothering"—good or bad—as it has been experienced since the beginning of time. The way the mother archetype manifests itself in a particular individual depends on personal factors like one's experience of the parents and the environment. This is the so-called mother complex, and if it's dubbed "negative," say, that's simply descriptive of its conse-

---

[18] *A Psychological Interpretation of the Golden Ass of Apuleius,* pp. 71-72.

quences in one's life to date. But no need to fear, your savior lurks in the wings: the opposite, which dwells in you. You only need to get in touch with the other side of the archetype.

No wonder, then, that when you deal with complexes analytically you have to stand on your head.

"There is no energy without the tension that naturally exists between opposites," said Adam. "So in cases of depression, for instance, it is necessary to discover the opposite to the attitude of the conscious mind. The shadow, seen from the one-sided point of view of ego-consciousness, is an inferior or threatening component of the personality and is consequently repressed in favor of a more comfortable or familiar self-image, the persona. The repressed unconscious contents must be made conscious so as to produce a tension of opposites, without which life cannot flow."

He picked up Jung's *Two Essays* and read:

> The conscious mind is on top, the shadow underneath, and just as high always longs for low and hot for cold, so all consciousness, perhaps without being aware of it, seeks its unconscious opposite, lacking which it is doomed to stagnation, congestion and ossification. Life is born only of the spark of opposites.[19]

I peeked at my watch. My appointment at the vet was for nine. It was now a quarter to and Sunny was tugging at my pants.

"I have to go," I said apologetically.

"Must you? Yes, of course," said Adam. "Would you like to come back for the TV session? . . . Oh, never mind, I dare say I can manage. But if you feel like it and have the time . . ."

Adam actually looked forlorn. Was it possible, after all, that he needed me as much as I needed him?

"I'll be here," I promised.

After dropping Sunny at the vet I called Rachel. She was working on a new piece, a mixed media collage—paint, fabric, wood, encaustic, spectrafoil. I see her things at various stages. It's all chaos to me, until one day presto!—everything comes together. I don't know how she does it, but then that's what she says about my stuff too.

---

[19] "The Problem of the Attitude-Type," CW 7, par. 78.

"How's Mr. Cabiri?" she asked. She said it fondly, referring to Jung's notion that the little people in dreams and visions are akin to the diminutive helpers of Hephaestus, blacksmith to the gods.[20]

"He's in great spirits. He asked after you too. The winsome Rachel, a delicate touch with a brush; that's just what he said."

"The rascal. Your book?"

"Coming along, thanks. What's up with J.K.?"

"Oh, you know, I don't see her all that much. She hangs out with her friends, in trees."

"We're all apes at heart," I said.

Rachel laughed. "And in other places too."

We rang off and I spent a couple of hours on details. I took the messages off the answering machine, wrote a few checks and updated the mailing list. I did the laundry, and while I was in the basement I checked the inventory and made notes for reprints and other supplies. I watered the plants, washed the dishes, made a grocery list. I vacuumed the pool and swept the deck. I made myself a corned beef sandwich with Dijon mustard and garlic pickles, and ate it with a knuckle of Johnny Walker. This is my life, I thought. I was thrilled.

Being Saturday there was no new mail, but there were a couple of letters I hadn't yet answered. This one came from England:

Dear Sir/Madam,

I would be very pleased if you would accept my typed scripts for publishing. My typed scripts is about my nasty experience of school bullying which included a broken finger. The name of the unruly thug who broke my finger at M— school is named as J—. If you are interested I will send you my typed scripts to read and would be grateful if you would give me a definite answer.

I am a sucker for heart-felt pleas. Others may fill their waste-baskets without a second thought. I answer almost everything, and especially a soul in distress. I am waylaid by concern for who's at the other end.

---

[20] "The Cabiri are . . . the mysterious creative powers, the gnomes who work under the earth, i.e., below the threshold of consciousness, in order to supply us with lucky ideas. As imps and hobgoblins, however, they play all sorts of nasty tricks." ("A Psychological Approach to the Dogma of the Trinity," *Psychology and Religion,* CW 11, par. 244)

That's a positive mother complex for you. How to respond to this woman's letter, however, still stumped me, so again I put it aside. Maybe I would send it to my friend whose Zürich thesis was called *The Wounded Finger: Anchorage for Soul and Sense.*

The other one was from Seoul, Korea:

> To Whom It May Concern,
>
> I extend to you my best greetings and wishes for prosperity.
>
> I am writing to you about the results of my research on the female sexual anatomy. After more than thirty years of studies I have developed a method by which it is possible to easily recognize those women whose sexual organs are able to provide the greatest pleasure to a man.
>
> By the form of the facial lips one can distinguish whether a woman has one of the extremely rare "ideal types" of sexual organ (so to speak, the Gold, Silver and Bronze medals among the sexual organs), or one of twenty other excellent types I have classified (see attached material).
>
> I am sure that my book *Lips and Sex* can sell millions of copies within months. The need for it is great, and I would be glad if your company would be interested in publishing it in English.

Enclosed were graphic descriptions of the sensory delights a man would experience on entering each of the three medal-winning vaginas described by the ancient Chinese—the "Thousand Worms" type, the "Millet on the Ceiling" type and the "Pouch with a String" type—plus a rare fourth, the "Gentle Chew" type, discovered by the author himself. It was a colorful quaternity.

I had initially dismissed this with a laugh. I don't publish that kind of book, and anyway I already had an open invitation to a medal winner. So why hadn't I trashed the letter? Maybe my shadow was interested.

Indeed, he said now, "What's to lose?"

"Only my reputation," I replied.

"Aw, gimme a break," he said.

Together we wrote back:

> Dear Sir,
>
> Congratulations on your research into matters that have intrigued men for centuries. We would very much like to see a copy of your manuscript. Is it on computer disk?

Then I stared at the wall.

It was now twenty years since I came back from Zürich with so much energy I thought I might explode. J.K. told me the other day that she read of people who suddenly, spontaneously combust. It's hard to believe, but theoretically it's possible. $E = MC^2$. If you had no place to put your energy, it could build up inside until poof!—a burst of flame and at the speed of light you're toast. In my case, however, it was more likely that I would float away into the sky and end up on some interplanetary rock like St. Exupéry's Little Prince, who fell in love with a flower and whose best friend was a fox.

I was puffed up with learning; I knew things others didn't.

Circumstances, and Rachel, kept me down to earth. Among the former was a divorce. That took considerable energy, and so did finding a place to live, setting up a practice, giving lectures and seminars. But there was still lots left and I put it into publishing books. First my Diploma thesis[21] —because no one else would do it—and then, because I didn't fancy being a one-shot vanity press, I invited manuscripts from others. The rest, as they say, is history.

Rachel, now what can I say about Rachel? Well, if she didn't exist I would certainly have to invent her. But in fact she was there from the beginning, only I didn't know it. I became aware of her as a phantom mate who wanted attention and put me in a bad mood when she didn't get it. So we talked and laughed and quarreled and made up, and then did it all again, and again, and over time we developed a workable relationship.

Actually, her name wasn't Rachel at first; it was Diane, my teen-age love and for years the girl of my dreams. Then she was Gladys, my secretary at P & G, then Anna, then Charlotte, and for a few weeks Nicole, a white witch whose erotic repertoire included the butterfly waltz and the Mulungi shuffle. For three passionate months in Zürich she was Cynthia. Ah, Cynthia, a real street fighter, that one; she told me she'd spent half her childhood hiding from her father in the laundry basket. There were others along the way; so many, so brief, I forget their names. But finally she was, and remains, my Rachel.

Of course that's all inside.

---

[21] *The Secret Raven: Conflict and Transformation in the Life of Franz Kafka.*

The other Rachel, mother of J.K., is flesh and blood. Call her Rachel Two. From the beginning we have had a lively connection based on lust and mutual respect, but I often wonder if it would have survived if I had not gotten to know her name-sake first—and she, perhaps, mine. At first I couldn't tell my Rachels apart, and sometimes I still mistake one for the other—and who doesn't, I'd like to know—but when I do they set me straight. I imagine it's like having two mistresses, though personally I wouldn't know, being a one-woman man—well, at any one time. Maybe that's what's behind my interest in the Don Juan syndrome. Think of going from one bed to another, and then some! And well received wherever! Boy-o, boy-o, as Adam might say. My shadow would jump at that. *Lips and Sex.* But how does one keep it up? Not indefinitely, it seems.

J.K. was an accident, or so we thought at the time. I was ambivalent at first; Rachel Two was not. I already had three others out in the world; she had none. She was adamant; she'd go the distance with or without me. Then Rachel One weighed in. Abandon her, she said, and I leave you. I took this to heart. So the three of us went to breathing classes and at the home-birth I was one of the midwives. For sixteen hours we took turns walking Rachel Two back and forth. I worked my way through a bottle of Chivas Regal while the doctor snoozed on the couch, and when Jessy Kate popped out she was quite as welcome as if she'd been planned. Now we can't imagine life without her. And that's no accident.

My Rachels still have their own agendas, and I mine. We like it that way because it works.

Okay. So the energy I left Zürich with has had considerable issue. But as a matter of fact it's been waning recently. I don't greet the day with my old enthusiasm. I'm not so interested in what's in the box. Why not? I have everything I ever wanted, and more.

The good, says Jung, is the enemy of the better. "If better is to come, good must step aside."[22] I've experienced the truth of that and I've often quoted it to others to encourage an openness to a nagging, underlying po-

---

22 "The Development of Personality," *The Development of Personality,* CW 17, par. 320. This idea was not original with Jung; Goethe said something similar: "If ever in this world we reach what's good / We call what's better just a plain falsehood!" (*Faust, Part I,* "The Night Scene")

tential, a blind leap from a so-so life to the unknown. But when you already have the best life you can think of, what could possibly be better?

Maybe that's the point. Me, my ego, thinks all is for the best. But something or someone, in me, has another point of view. Maybe I haven't been paying enough attention to my other parts. Now there's a thought. What do they want?

My dream last night, galloping through the forest. So many trees; I can't see the forest for them. I put my mind to that. As if I had a choice; as if I were in charge.

4
Adam's Fling with Fame

I returned to Adam's just after two. He told me that he'd tidied up, being house-proud, but the only difference I could see was that the spines of the magazines were even and not higgledy-piggledy. He'd also dressed up. He looked quite elegant in a sky-blue suit and mauve bow-tie. His few strands of hair were neatly brushed, nails clipped, goatee trimmed, feet shod in ankle-high Bally boots, ox-blood.

"Spiffy," I said.

"There are times when one must cater to the projections of others," said Adam. "A learned gentleman does not sport an apron and sandals on TV. I have other personas in the closet. Would you care to see some?"

He was regaling me with anecdotes of his hunting days in Borneo when the TV crew arrived. The crew was two: a wiry fellow hoisting a camera, and a slim young lady in a bolero vest and flowered skirt. She introduced herself as the director and interviewer.

"Rickster, Ima T.," she said, vigorously shaking our hands. "This here is Ben. Thank God for Ben; he's handy, I'm not!"

She looked around. "My, what a great place! It has ambiance. Did you do it all by yourself?"

Ben was about thirty, boyish, in jeans and a black tee-shirt that asked: **Do You Know Where I Was Last Night?**

"Pleased to meet you," he waved. He put the camera down and backed out. He returned in a minute with spotlights and a coil of electrical cable. He busied himself setting up.

"Tea? Coffee?" I offered.

Ima T. Rickster said she'd prefer a Diet Coke. Ben said if it was not too much trouble he wouldn't mind a cold beer. I found one of each in Adam's fridge.

"Professor Brillig!" gushed Ms. Rickster, "I have to tell you, this is such an honor."

Adam bowed.

"As I told you on the phone," she said, "I work freelance. One day radio, the next TV, and in between I write an article or two. It's a fun life, always something new, learning on the job, just one step ahead. Well you guys know that, I'm sure. I bet you hear a lot of secrets too!

"I saw you last year when you spoke on the archetypal significance of Chicken Little. I was on assignment and I didn't know an archetype from a toothbrush! I don't suppose you'd remember, but I'm the one who asked if Chicken Little might be called the first feminist. You said it was conceivable if she were female, otherwise unlikely. I thought that was priceless! Remember?

"Well, maybe you read my catchy review. 'Jungian analyst Adam Brillig emerged from retirement last night to stun a capacity audience in Great Hall by equating Chicken Little's Cassandra-like odyssey with the Grail legend.' And so on. Je-sus! Did I get razzed about that! Of course my editor cut it to shreds, though he left in your comparison of Ms. Little—you're *such* a gentleman—with the Christ-stone rejected by the builders. What did you mean by that, anyway? Is it really true? Oh, but you were brilligant!"

She was waltzing along the path as she talked, twirling her skirt and fingering leaves. Her eyes darted from side to side. She stopped at a cage and exclaimed. "Axolotls?! For goodness sakes! What do they eat?"

She meandered back to where we still stood. "Hey Ben, let's go, we don't have all day."

Ben looked up from where he was, on all fours. He smiled at her and addressed Adam. "Sir, I am looking for wall-plugs."

Adam scratched his head and said he thought there were some behind the foliage.

"Now where shall we sit," mused Ms. Rickster, looking around.

Adam and I exchanged glances.

"Dear lady," said Adam, "I have the world on a string. Let me give you one end."

With a flourish he produced a length of rope which he proceeded to loop and tie around her waist. The other end he tied to a hot-water radiator. He then presented her with a stool.

"There now," said Adam. "If you stay more or less in one place we can talk. For my part, I would prefer the freedom to range."

Ima T. Rickster was delighted.

"Ben, did you hear that? Jeez, get a move on, man, this should all be on film."

It took another ten minutes to get the lighting right, but finally everything was in place. Adam straightened his tie and composed himself cross-legged on a cushion. Ben lowered a sound-boom between them. Ms. Rickster dipped into a make-up case and buffed Adam's face and head with a powdered pom-pom.

"There now," she said, "you want your words to shine, not your pate, right? You dear old dear old dear. Trust me, I've done this a hundred times."

She primped herself in a mirror and then looked at her notes. "Are you ready?" she said to Adam.

He nodded.

"Ben?" she called.

Ben poked his head out from behind the camera. "Could you move just a little closer together?"

Adam inched his cushion toward Ms. Rickster's stool. Ms. Rickster inched her stool toward Adam's cushion.

Ben said, "Hold it . . . focusing . . . yeah, okay . . . rolling."

Whirrr.

"Good evening. My name is Ima T. Rickster and this is *People in Places,* brought to you by your neighbors in education, the *Encyclopedia Americana.* Looking for information? Well we've got it and you can have it. See the numbers rolling along the bottom of your screen? That's us. Give us a ring, toll-free outside Metro, except, we're sorry, we can't pay for your call from a cell-phone.

"My guest tonight is Professor Adam Brillig, author and explorer, analyst emeritus, an octogenarian of small stature, reputed wisdom and great charm." She smiled at Adam. "Good things come in small packages, I always say."

He glowed. She continued.

"I am speaking from Professor Brillig's aerie in Metro, a jungle of learning, truly a cornucopia of a lived life." She paused. "Or is it? Look around! Is this an illusion, these exotic plants and animals, these prints and paintings, these cards and books; or do they really comprise a compendium of the human mind, a summation of civilization as we know it? And Prof. Brillig himself, this little fellow with an engaging limp, is he simply, as some say, an eccentric old dwarf with a few wisps of hair . . ."

Adam started up. She stilled him with a stern look.

". . . or is he the unheralded genius others claim him to be—a gimp, yes, but one who from humble beginnings and in the face of sizeism has topped his profession and garnered numerous accolades for his pioneering work in the barnyard?"

She paused again. Adam readied himself.

"Well folks," said Ms. Rickster, "we know where we stand, but now it's your say. You out there, what do *you* think? We want to hear from you, and we're waiting! See the numbers rolling along the bottom of your screen? That's us. Give us a ring, toll-free outside Metro, except, we're sorry, we can't pay for your call from a cell-phone.

"Thanks for being there from *Encyclopedia Americana,* your neighbors in education. Looking for information? Well we've got it and you can have it. We'll be right back after this brief message."

"Cut," she said. "Good stuff, Ben, that's a wrap."

She put her clip-board down and smiled at Adam. "That wasn't too bad, was it? A piece of cake, really. Now if someone will just help me out of this truss . . ."

The lights went off. Ben started packing up. Adam didn't move. I untied Ms. Rickster and pulled her aside.

"Now look here," I whispered, "what about Adam?"

She looked blank. "What about Adam what?"

"You know, his song and dance."

"Oh that. It's all in the can. Stock footage."

"And when people call in?"

"We have the answers. Trust me, I've done this a hundred times."

"So why did you come?"

She looked at me as if I were daft.

"Because he was here," she said.

5
Deep Throat

I sat by Adam as the light faded. When he stirred I helped him up and steered him to a stool in the kitchen. I brewed a pot of tea and set out some cheese and biscuits. I opened a tin of oysters and in the cupboard I found some olives and his stash of caviar. It all made a nice plate.

Adam sighed. "I should have known better."

He looked older.

The phone rang. I answered. It was Rachel. "Hi, how did it go?"

"About as well as could be expected," I said. I gave her the scene in a few sentences.

"I'm sorry," said Rachel. "Are you still on for dinner?"

"If you don't mind I'd like to stay awhile with Adam."

"Okay, I will pick up Sunny. J.K. says to say Hi and she loves you. Me too."

"Listen," I said, "Sunny collapsed again last night going up stairs. I forgot to tell the vet."

"I'll check it out," said Rachel.

Adam had some color back. We snacked for a time in silence.

"I was ready," he said. "I was half awake all night rehearsing."

I suddenly had an idea.

"Let's play pretend," I said. "I'll ask questions as if I were a reporter, and you speak your mind as if you were Jung."

"That's goofy," said Adam morosely. "It's not real."

Goofy. This from a man known to stand on his head and recite the Jabberwocky. A man who counseled people to talk to the wall. A man who idolized a chicken.

"It's real enough to me," I said. "Look, I need material for my book. Are you in or out?"

Adam made a face and I thought I was done for. Then he got up and rummaged in a cupboard. He came back with a turnip.

"Let's pretend it's radio." He managed a smile. "Here's your mike."

Now that's the spirit, I thought. We piled the dishes in the sink and went back to the cushions. Adam got out his pipe and I rolled a cigarette. I found a pad of paper and for a few minutes made notes. Adam hummed "Who's Afraid of the Big Bad Wolf," or maybe that was me.

"Ready?" I asked, when I was.

"Let's do it," said Adam.

I am not handy with root vegetables, but when I found a way to hold the turnip I thrust it at his face. I tried to look serious.

"Hello out there," I said, in my best mid-Atlantic voice. "I am with Professor C.G. Jung." And to Adam: "Or Carl, may I?"

He nodded. "Why not."

"Perhaps," I said, "you could start by describing your feelings about Sigmund Freud. It is well known that you were friends and colleagues for some years. What happened?"

Adam looked at the ceiling.

"It is true," he said, "that I started out entirely in agreement with Freud. I was even considered to be his best disciple. We were on excellent terms until I had the idea that certain things were symbolical. Freud would not agree to this, and furthermore he identified his method with the theory and the theory with the method. To my mind that is impossible. You cannot identify a method with science. But I am perfectly well aware of the merits of Freud and I would not wish to diminish them. I know that what he says agrees with many people, and I assume that these people have the kind of psychology he describes. Adler, who has entirely different views, also has a large following, and I am convinced that many people have an Adlerian psychology, so to speak. Now I too have a following, which presumably consists of people who have a psychology similar to mine."

"Would you say, then," I asked, "that your contribution to psychology is, how shall I put it . . . subjective?"

"Of course; it is entirely subjective. It is my personal psychology, my prejudice, that determines how I see psychological facts. I readily admit that I see things in such and such a way. Why don't Freud and Adler do the same—confess that their ideas are their subjective point of view? We all instinctively have certain points of view. It would be neurotic if I saw things in another way than my instinct tells me to; my snake, as the primitives say, would be all against me. When Freud said certain things, my snake did not agree. And I must take the route my snake prescribes, because that is good for me."

He closed in on the turnip.

"Mind you," he said, "I have patients with whom I am obliged to go into all the details of sex and childhood that Freud has described. I have other cases that force me to an Adlerian point of view because they have a power complex."

"What is the difference?" I asked.

"Well," said Adam, "people who have the capacity to adapt and are successful are more inclined to have a Freudian psychology, because someone in that position is looking for the gratification of desires. Those who have not been successful don't have the time to think about desires, or rather they have only one—the desire to succeed; they will have an Adlerian psychology with all the earmarks of a power complex.

"Personally, I don't have a power complex because I have been fairly successful and in nearly every respect I have been able to adapt. If the whole world disagrees with me I am perfectly indifferent. I have a good place to live, I enjoy myself, and if nobody reads my books it doesn't matter to me. I know nothing better than being in my library, and if I make a few discoveries that is wonderful."

"And your desires, Professor—you have had some?"

Adam chuckled.

"Quite a lot," he said, "but I never had difficulties with desires in the Freudian sense. As a boy I lived in the country and took things very naturally. The unnatural things of which Freud speaks were not interesting to me. To talk of an incest complex just bores me to tears. But I know exactly how I could make myself neurotic: if I said or believed something that is not myself. I say what I see, and others can take it or leave it. In all conscience I can adhere to neither the Freudian nor the Adlerian point of view. I can agree only with the Jungian approach to the psyche because I see things that way even if there is not a single person on earth who shares my views. The only thing I can hope for is to present some interesting ideas and let people see how I tackle things."

"Do you think your way is right, or better?" I asked.

"Right? Better?" smiled Adam. "Who knows? I once belonged to a church whose minister put the Ten Commandments on one side and Satan on the other. Black and white. He knew his opposites all right; they were cut and dried, with no bridge between. My experience is that life is gray. I now say, know who you are and guide yourself accordingly. The difficulty is in knowing who you are.

"Most people confuse self-knowledge with knowledge of their conscious ego-personalities. The real psychic facts are for the most part hidden. Anyone who has any ego-consciousness at all takes it for granted that he knows himself. But the ego knows only its own contents, which are largely dependent on social factors. There is also the unconscious and its contents, and without some knowledge of them one cannot claim to know oneself. In this respect the psyche behaves like the body, of whose physiological and anatomical structure the average person knows little. We are accustomed to take steps against physical infection. Similarly, we can guard against the risk of psychic infection, but only when we know what is attacking us, and how, where and when the attack might come."

This was meaty. No matter how often I read Jung or discuss his ideas, I am always struck by something new. I encouraged Adam to continue.

"How," I asked, "does one acquire self-knowledge?"

"It is a matter of getting to know the individual facts," he said, "your own individual facts. Theories are of little help, for the more a theory lays claim to universal validity, the less capable it is of doing justice to the individual facts. Any theory based on experience is necessarily statistical; it formulates an ideal average which abolishes the exceptions at either end of the scale and replaces them by an abstract mean. The mean may be quite valid without ever occurring in reality. The exceptions at either extreme, though equally factual, do not appear in the final result since they cancel each other out.

"If, for instance, I determine the weight of each stone in a pile of pebbles and get an average weight of five ounces, this tells me very little about the nature of any particular pebble. Anyone who might think, on the basis of these findings, to pick up a pebble of five ounces on the first try would be in for a serious disappointment. Indeed, there might not be a single pebble in the whole pile weighing exactly five ounces. That is the reality of statistics and of theories based on them. The distinctive thing about facts, however, is their individuality. One might even say that the real picture consists of nothing but exceptions to the rule. For this reason I believe that there can be no self-knowledge based on theoretical assumptions. The object of the knowledge, oneself, is unique and singular—a relative exception and an irregular phenomenon.

"Similarly, in the treatment of psychic suffering, I have always stressed that the so-called scientific knowledge of humankind in general must take second place; the important thing is the particular person. On the one hand we are equipped with statistical truths, and on the other we are faced with someone who requires individual understanding. I do not deny the validity of the former, but the more schematic the treatment, the more resistances it calls up in the patient; and quite rightly, too, for the individual facts are the essential element. The analyst therefore needs to have a kind of two-way thinking: doing one thing while not losing sight of the other."

"Why do you think depth psychology is a new way to acquire self-knowledge?" I asked.

"Because," said Adam, "all the methods previously practiced did not take into account the existence of the unconscious. This new factor in our field of vision has seriously complicated and fundamentally altered how we go about knowing ourselves. It is clear now that we are twofold beings; we have a conscious side which we more or less know, and an unconscious side of which we know little but which is no secret to others. Think of how often we make all sorts of mistakes without being aware of them in the least, while others suffer them all the more painfully."

I said: "You mean, like, our one hand doesn't know what the other is doing?"

"Even so," nodded Adam. "The recognition of the existence of an unconscious side of ourselves is of revolutionary importance. Conscience, for instance, as an ethical authority extends only as far as consciousness extends. When we lack knowledge of our other side, we can do the most astonishing things, the most terrible, without calling ourselves to account and without ever suspecting what we're doing. Unconscious actions are always taken for granted and therefore not critically evaluated. We are then surprised at the incomprehensible reactions of others, who hold us to be responsible. Instead of questioning ourselves, we seek in others the cause of all the consequences that follow from our own actions. The increased self-knowledge that comes about through depth psychology allows you both to remedy your own mistakes and to become more understanding of others."

"Do you think self-knowledge of the kind you've described can have a healing effect?" I asked.

"That is my experience," said Adam.

"Can it happen without analysis?"

Adam rubbed his nose.

"I suppose, to some extent," he said, "if you are alert to the effects of your behavior on your environment and willing to learn from them. But even so, knowledge of ourselves is blinkered by our blind-spots and by the silence of others who for one reason or another indulge us. To really get a handle on ourselves we need an honest, objective mirror. Our intimates are rarely that. Analysts are trained and equipped for the task.

"Historically, as you know, repentance, confession and purification from sin have been the conditions of salvation. That has traditionally been the province of religion, and still is, but among unbelievers the role is filled by depth psychology. As far as analysis helps confession, it can bring about a kind of renewal. Again and again I have found that patients dream of analysis as a refreshing and purifying bath, or their dreams and visions present symbols of rebirth. The knowledge of what's going on in their unconscious and its meaningful integration into their lives give them renewed vitality, as if they had been delivered from an otherwise unavoidable disaster, or from entanglement in the fickle skeins of fate."

I wondered aloud about the variety of methods and techniques espoused by therapists of different schools, but Adam cut me off.

"Technique is not important," he said. "What matters is the analyst's self-knowledge and attention to the unconscious. No doubt you have seen a craftsman at work. His skill makes the charm of a craft. Analysis is a craft and I deal in my individual way with the things I have to do. I think any decent analyst, trained in whatever school, does the same. When a unique, suffering person is in front of me, I put theory on the shelf and listen. Nor do I insist on analyzing the unconscious. Consistent support of the conscious attitude is often enough to bring about satisfactory results. So long as it does not obtrude itself, the unconscious is best left alone. Depth analysis is rather like a surgical operation; one should only resort to the knife when other methods have failed.

"Nobody is absolutely right in psychological matters. We must never forget that in psychology the means by which we judge and observe the psyche is the psyche itself. Did you ever hear of a hammer beating itself? In psychology the observer is the observed. The psyche is not only the object but also the subject. It is a vicious circle and we have to be very modest in what we claim to do. The best I can expect of other psychologists is that they put their cards on the table and admit: 'I handle things in such and such a way; this is how I see them because that's the way I am.' Then we can compare notes."

"Surely," I said, "there are some objective guidelines."

Adam laughed so hard he almost fell off his cushion.

"There is total chaos in psychology," he said. "There are so many theories that it is hard to be serious about any one. The Freudian and Adlerian schools are only the most well known of the depth psychologies. There is the Kleinian school and the Kohutians; there are Reichians, Lacanians, Hillmanians and Mindellians; there are those who work with sand, paint, clay, smells, bumps on the head; others still put their faith in abreaction or hypnosis. That is only in the psychodynamic area; there are also behaviorists, neurologists, physicists, linguists, theologians and philosophers who call themselves psychologists. Psychology is not a religious creed but a point of view."

This was provocative, but I wanted to return to an earlier issue.

"You do acknowledge," I said, "that some people are troubled sexually or have difficulty with power?"

"Indeed," said Adam, "and others have other troubles. I have mostly other troubles. My problem is to wrestle with the big monster of the historical past, the great snake of the centuries, the burden of the human mind, and particularly the problem of Christianity. It would be so much simpler if I knew nothing, but I know too much, through my ancestors and my education. Other people are not worried by such problems; they don't care about the historical burdens Christianity has heaped on us. But there are people who are concerned with the great battle between the present and the past or the future, and I am one of them. Some people make history and others build a little house in the suburbs. The world is huge and there is no one theory that explains everything."

I pressed on.

"According to Freud," I said, "the unconscious is chiefly a receptacle for childhood things we've repressed."

"Yes," said Adam. "He looked at it from the corner of the nursery. To me the unconscious is a vast historical warehouse. I have a nursery too, but it is small in comparison with the great spaces of history which have always been more interesting to me. Once I thought there were no people like myself. I thought it was megalomania to think as I did. Then I found many who agreed with my point of view, and I was satisfied that I represented at least some people whose basic psychological facts are expressed more or less aptly by my formulations. But I am not an intellectual tyrant. When I am not sure about a patient I suggest books by Freud and Adler and others and I say, 'Make a choice,' in order to see if we are on the right track. Sometimes we aren't, and it is good to know that."

He rocked on his heels and wiggled his ears.

"Come on," he said, "give me a hard one."

"To whom," I shot back, "do you think your views appeal?"

Adam sucked on his pipe.

"As a rule," he said, "to those who have reached a certain maturity and are philosophically minded, fairly successful in life and not too neurotic. They have conflicts and problems in relationships, but on the whole they are no sicker than the rest of us. They are grateful to learn about the influence of the unconscious and open to an historical and mythological perspective on their situation."

I cupped my hand over the turnip and whispered, "Well done!" Then I fed him another: "Freud spoke of the Id as a part of the unconscious. What's your view of that?"

Again Adam laughed.

"Jaundiced. I mean, why give it such a funny name? It is the unconscious and that's something we don't know. Of course the difference in our temperaments has produced a different outlook. You know, I never could bring myself to be so interested in sex cases. There are people with a neurotic sex life and you have to talk sex stuff with them until you're both sick of it and then finally you get out of that boredom. I like to get through all that as soon as possible so we can get on with more important things, like why they did what they did yesterday, and how they think and feel about that. Any taboo, as sex has certainly been, is the receptacle for all sorts of projections, but very often the real problem is not to be found there at all. Many people make unnecessary difficulties about sex when their actual troubles are of quite a different nature."

"Herr Professor," I said—I could not bring myself to address him less formally, if only to remind myself that deference was due the examined life—"perhaps you could give us an example?"

Adam reflected.

"Once a young man of about thirty, obviously clever and highly intellectual, came to me with a compulsion neurosis. He spent hours a day washing his hands, clothes, utensils, anything he touched. He brought a manuscript of his, a hundred and forty pages, a psychoanalytical autobiography which he said contained the history and analysis of his case.

" 'Will you read this,' he asked, "and tell me why I am not cured although I have had a complete analysis?'

"I agreed to read his material. It was an excellent scientific treatise based on a thorough study of the literature. It was quite perfect according to all the rules, good enough to be published.

"At our next meeting I congratulated him and said, 'I don't understand it either. You ought to be cured, but when you say you are not I have to believe you.'

"He said, 'Do you agree I have a complete insight into the structure of my neurosis?'

" 'I cannot fault your thesis,' I said. 'The whole thing is marvelously well demonstrated. There remains only one question, perhaps quite foolish. You don't mention where you came from or who your parents are. You say you winter on the Riviera and spend the summer in St. Moritz. Tell me, are your parents wealthy?'

" 'Not at all,' he said.

"'Oh, you have a successful business?'

" 'No, I don't work.'

" 'Ah, you have inherited a fortune from a rich uncle.'

" 'No.'

"I was puzzled. 'Then where does your money come from?'

" 'I have a certain arrangement,' he said, 'with a friend.'

" 'He must be a wonderful friend.'

" 'It is a woman,' he said.

"Well, then the full story came out. The women was considerably older than him. She was forty-six, a teacher with a small salary in an elementary school. She had fallen in love with this fellow at a dance-hall. Presumably she stinted herself so he could live the high life, while she naturally hoped in time to marry, an event this man was not remotely contemplating.

" 'And you ask why you are not cured!' I said to him.

"He replied: 'Oh, you have a moralistic point of view, and that is not at all scientific.'

"I said: 'Science be damned. Is it possible that you are are not yet cured because you are supported by this poor woman?'

"He protested: 'No, we agreed upon it. I had a serious talk with her and it is not a matter for discussion.'

"I said: 'Huh. Talk means nothing. You are pretending to yourself that it is not her money, but you live by it and that is immoral. That is the cause of your compulsion neurosis. It is a compensation; your psyche is punishing you for having an immoral attitude.'

To me Adam said: "This man stole a simple woman's life savings in order to have a good time. He deserved his neurosis, you see, for acting like a pig. He was unclean and he knew it. And that's why he couldn't stop washing. He was one of those who believe that morals have nothing to do with neurosis, that sinning on purpose is not sinning at all because it can be rationalized out of existence."

"Did that not come out in the analysis?" I asked.

"What analysis? I never saw him again. He left in a huff, saying anyone else would have been impressed by his interesting case instead of looking for simple explanations. He belongs in jail, and his compulsion neurosis provides it for him all right."[23]

"You *are* moralistic, then?"

"I? No more than anyone else," said Adam. "But understand, we are not talking here of a particular moral code, a socially sanctioned way of behavior. The psyche has a natural morality. It is simply this: what is right and true for this person at this time? The psyche is self-regulating, you see. It knows when you act like a scoundrel, and it tells you. If you don't get the message consciously, you will get it some other way. No one else may know, but your psyche exacts an appropriate price."

"Could you not make him see that?"

Adam shrugged.

"Naturally I try to do my best for my patients, but it is very important that one should not strive to heal at all costs. One has to be careful not to impose one's own will and conviction on the patient. You cannot wrest people away from their fate, just as in medicine you can't cure someone if nature means that person to die. Sometimes it is really a question whether you are allowed to rescue people from the fate they must undergo for the sake of their further development. We only develop psychologically by accepting ourselves as we are and by being serious enough to live the lives we have. Our sins and errors and mistakes are necessary, otherwise we are deprived of the most precious incentives to change.

"So when this young man went away, having heard something that might have changed his life, and did not pay attention, I did not call him back. Am I un-Christian for that? Perhaps, but I am not in the business of saving people from themselves. I am on the side of nature. The old Chinese Book of Wisdom says: 'The Master says it once.' He does not run after people. Those who are meant to hear will understand, and those who are not meant to understand will not hear."

---

[23] I subsequently came upon a similar case described by Jung in two places ("Analytical Psychology and Education," *The Development of Personality,* CW 17, pars. 182f., and "The Tavistock Lectures," *The Symbolic Life,* CW 18, pars. 282ff.) Others might call this an example of cryptomnesia, or hidden memory, whereby something long forgotten comes to mind, without the original source (so that it seems to be one's own), but I think Adam knew what he was doing. I had asked him to pretend he was Jung, and he did.

I was silent for a minute; then I said: "I'd like to clarify a very elementary point."

"Please, don't be shy," said Adam.

"What is your working definition of neurosis?"

Adam considered. Maybe this was the hard one.

"A good deal of neurosis," he said finally, "is intimately bound up with the problems of our time; it really represents an unsuccessful attempt to solve general problems in one's own person. Without being aware of it, the neurotic participates in the dominant cultural currents of the age and reflects them in a personal conflict. Neurosis is self-division. In most people the cause of the division is that the conscious mind wants to hold on to its moral ideal, while the unconscious strives after its—in the contemporary sense—unmoral ideal, which the conscious mind tries to deny. People of this type want to be more respectable than they really are. The young man I spoke of is a case in point.

"But the conflict can easily be the other way around. There are those who to all appearances are disreputable and do not restrain themselves in the least. This is at bottom only a pose of wickedness, for behind that is their moral side which has fallen into the unconscious, just as surely as the immoral side has in the moral person. Both feel the pinch of the shadow."

It was now well past midnight and I was finding it increasingly hard to keep my eyes open.

Adam noticed and said: "I have more to say on this, but you, my friend, have had the biscuit. Stay again, won't you? I do like this conceit; it gets my blood going. But it needs two to play. Here, the honeymoon suite is still warm . . ."

And so for the second night in a row I found myself on Adam's cot. I was rather excited about the evening's work. I wished my Rachel-artist was there to share it with, but not for long because her step-sister, Rachel One, was.

6
Neurosis and the Self-Regulating Psyche

"A neurosis," said Adam, "is a dissociation of the personality due to the existence of complexes."

It was 7 a.m. and we were at it again. The few birds that hadn't gone south were chirping. I had a cup of coffee in one hand and the trusty turnip in the other. Adam was in a velvet dressing gown, dunking dry toast in herbal tea.

"To have complexes," he said, "is in itself normal; but if they are incompatible, that part of the personality which is too contrary to the conscious part becomes split off. If the split reaches the organic structure, the dissociation is a psychosis—a schizophrenic condition. Each complex then lives a life of its own, with no ego left to hold the parts together.

"Since the split-off complexes are unconscious, they find only an indirect means of expression, through symptoms. Instead of consciously suffering through a conflict, then, one suffers from a neurosis. Any incompatibility of character can cause dissociation, and too great a split between the thinking and the feeling function, for instance, is already a slight neurosis. When you are not quite at one with yourself in a given matter at a given time, you are approaching a neurotic condition."

"Is everyone neurotic, then?" I asked.

"Of course," he laughed, "more or less. Who is undivided, conflict-free? Who is one? It is only a matter of degree. The idea of dissociation is the most general and cautious way I can define neurosis. Of course it doesn't cover the myriad ways in which neurosis manifests itself; it's just the most general psychological formulation I can give."

I scrambled to nail this down.

"Can we assume then, that you regard the outbreak of a neurosis as an attempt at self-cure, an attempt at compensation by, for instance, bringing out the inferior function?"

Adam nodded. "Absolutely."

"Are you saying," I persisted, "that neurosis, from the point of view of a person's development, is favorable?"

54

"Indeed," replied Adam. "In many cases we have to say, 'Thank goodness he could make up his mind to be neurotic.' It is far more promising than a murky borderline state.

"I truly believe that neurosis is an attempt at self-cure, just as any physical disease is partly that. We can no longer understand a disease as a thing-in-itself, as something detached, which not so long ago was the prevalent opinion. The whole person is involved. Modern medicine conceives of disease as a system composed of a harmful factor and a healing factor. It is exactly the same with neurosis. It is an attempt of the self-regulating psychic system to restore the balance, in no way different from the function of dreams, only rather more forceful and drastic."

I said: "I'm sure our listeners would be pleased to hear how you think this works."

"May I refer to Jung?" asked Adam coyly.

"Surely," I smiled.

"Well," said Adam, "Jung observed, as many others have, that in a psychological crisis unconscious contents become particularly active—dreams, memories, fantasies and so on. He interpreted this phenomenon as an attempt by the psyche itself to compensate the one-sided attitude of consciousness; that is, to present to the conscious mind information that would be helpful in resolving the crisis. This can happen at any age, but it is seldom necessary in the first half of life. The problems of young people generally come from a collision between the forces of reality and an inadequate, infantile attitude, characterized by an abnormal dependence on the parents. Therapy in such cases involves transferring the imagos of the parents onto more suitable substitute figures and techniques aimed at encouraging the development of a strong ego."

"So what happens," I asked, "when you already have a good ego? Say you've long since left the parental home and held down a job; you have a mate and maybe children of your own. Everything is going along fine, it seems, and then one day nothing works any more. You just want to hide in the closet. You have terrible moods, dark thoughts and suspicions; fantasies give you no peace. Your life is rosy but your outlook is bleak. You've lost your energy and ambition; you're anxious and feel you've missed the boat. There's nothing you can put your finger on, but life has no meaning. Where before you could cope, now you can't. You hurt and you think of suicide. What then, Professor, eh?"

I helped myself to a bagel and cream cheese.

"I was getting there," said Adam petulantly. "In later life a strong ego is precisely what stands in the way of further development. Do you remember Jung's dictum that the good is the enemy of the better? 'If better is to come, good must stand aside'?"

"Yes." I didn't tell him I'd already used it.

"It was Jung's belief," said Adam, "that in midlife psychological development no longer depends on the dissolution of infantile ties and illusions, but on coming to grips with the problem of opposites—the disparity between conscious attitudes and what is going on in the unconscious. The ability to hold the tension that arises in a conflict situation is of paramount importance, and for this a firm ego is essential. That is the basis for Jung's so-called synthetic, or purposive, view of neurosis."

"That's quite different," I noted, "from the Freudian view that psychological problems stem from Oedipal conflicts in early childhood."

"Yes," said Adam," but it isn't necessarily incompatible. It would be closer to the truth, I think, to say that the two views are complementary. Freud looked to the past for the cause of psychic discomfort in the present, while Jung focused on the present with an eye to what was possible in the future."

I sat back and thought of the people I knew. Those in analysis seemed to fit Jung's model, but I knew many others in midlife, close friends, relatives even, who hadn't broken down. So they hobbled a bit; their shiny persona was a tad rusty and they were easily upset by things they used to take in their stride. But they weren't on their knees.

I said to Adam: "It is still a mystery to me why one person goes to pieces, while someone else, perhaps in equally difficult circumstances, or even worse, doesn't."

He smiled.

"That's the 64,000 dollar question," he said. "Nobody knows for certain, but I think Jung would say that the individual psyche knows both its limits and its potential. If the limits are being exceeded, or the potential not realized, a breakdown occurs. Those who learn the symbolic language of the psyche come out of it with renewed energy; the rest stay stuck in a hole. And who is destined for which depends more on motivation and innate potential than on anything the analyst says or does. I'm not unhappy with that view."

His words sparked something in me; I suddenly wanted to be alone.

"I need a break," I whispered to Adam, and to the turnip: "Thank you, Professor. And you out there, you who hurt, with ears to hear—don't go away, we'll be right back after these words from our sponsor."

To Adam I said: "I'm not deserting you."

"Oh don't mind me," he said. "I have lots to do."

I called Rachel One, inside, and described where we were.

"Be careful," she cautioned, "you're getting into deep water."

Then I called Rachel Two.

"Speak up, I can't hear for the hammering." Damn, I'd forgotten she was in the midst of house repairs. This happens more often than I like. I get so caught up in my own stuff that I don't give a thought to others.

Rachel heard me out and said, "Go for it. By the way, the vet says not to worry about Sunny; she's just arthritic."

"That makes two of us," I grimaced.

Before going on with Adam I wanted to review a few things. Like any cub reporter, I was afraid of screwing up. That was one of the first things I learned in journalism (after the importance of the Five W's: who, what, why, when and where)—*Know your subject.* Now it's true that in this situation I wasn't sure whether my subject was Adam or Jung. Or it could have been myself, a possibility I didn't learn in journalism. That aside, my focus this day was on facts and theory pertaining to the neurotic personality. With this in mind I retired to the cot with a pile of books and over the next hour or so I cobbled together the following.

Jung did not dispute Freudian theory that Oedipal fixations can manifest in later life as neurosis. He agreed that certain periods in life, and particularly infancy, often have a permanent and determining influence on the personality. He simply pointed out that this was an insufficient explanation for those cases where there was no trace of a neurosis until the time of breakdown. Here's what he wrote:

If the fixation were indeed real [i.e., the primary cause] we should expect to find its influence constant; in other words, a neurosis lasting throughout life. This is obviously not the case. The psychological determination of a neurosis is only partly due to an early infantile predisposition; it must be due to some cause in the present as well. And if we carefully examine the kind of infantile fantasies and occurrences to which the neurotic is attached, we shall be obliged to agree that there is nothing in them that is specifically neurotic. Normal individuals have pretty much the same inner and outer experiences, and may be attached to them to an astonishing degree without developing a neurosis.[24]

Together with the hypothesis of fixation, Freud proposed that the incestuous desires of the Oedipus complex were the primary cause of the neurotic's characteristic regression to infantile fantasies. Jung accepted this for some years, but in 1913 he broke with the Vienna school when he introduced an energic viewpoint into the psychology of neurosis:

All psychological phenomena can be considered as manifestations of energy, in the same way that all physical phenomena have been understood as energic manifestations ever since Robert Mayer discovered the law of the conservation of energy. Subjectively and psychologically, this energy is conceived as *desire*. I call it *libido,* using the word in its original sense, which is by no means sexual. . . .

From a broader standpoint libido can be understood as vital energy in general, or as Bergson's *elan vital.*[25]

Ah, so here's the deep water. What is the connection between neurosis and energy?

Psychic events, suggests Jung, are analogous to physical events. Both can be viewed from either a mechanistic or an energic standpoint:

The mechanistic view is purely causal; it conceives an event as the effect of a cause, in the sense that unchanging substances change their relations to one another according to fixed laws. The energic point of view on the other hand is in essence final. . . . The flow of energy has a definite direction (goal) in that it follows the gradient of potential in a way that cannot be reversed.[26]

---

[24] "Psychoanalysis and Neurosis," *Freud and Psychoanalysis,* CW 4, par. 564.
[25] Ibid., pars. 567f.
[26] "On Psychic Energy," *The Structure and Dynamics of the Psyche,* CW 8, pars. 2f.

Jung felt that both views were valid, depending on the individual case: "Expediency, that is to say, the possibility of obtaining results, alone decides whether the one or the other view is to be preferred."[27]

With respect to neurosis, which both Jung and Freud saw in terms of a blockage of libido, the mechanistic or reductive view traces the problem back to a primary cause—namely, childhood factors—while the energic or final view asks what is the intention of the psyche as a whole; where does the energy "want" to go? As with Buridan's ass, what is it that one feels pushed toward?

Now, Jung builds on the idea that the principle of conservation of energy applies to the psyche as well as to the physical world. He refers to the principle of equivalence, the law in physics which states that for a given quantity of energy expended or consumed in bringing about a certain condition, an equal amount of the same or another form of energy will appear elsewhere. Psychologically, this means that where there is an overabundance of energy in one place, some other psychic function has been deprived; conversely, when libido "disappears," as it does in depression, it must appear in another form, for instance as a symptom. Jung writes:

> Every time we come across a person who has a "bee in his bonnet," or a morbid conviction, or some extreme attitude, we know that there is too much libido, and that the excess must have been taken from somewhere else where, consequently, there is too little. . . . Thus the symptoms of a neurosis must be regarded as exaggerated functions over-invested with libido.
>
> The question has to be reversed in the case of those syndromes characterized mainly by lack of libido, for instance apathetic states. Here we have to ask, where did the libido go? The libido is there, but it is not visible and is inaccessible to the patient himself. . . . It is the task of psychoanalysis to search out that hidden place where the libido dwells . . . . The hidden place is the "non-conscious," which we may also call the "unconscious" without attributing to it any mystical significance.[28]

While Jung acknowledged that reductive interpretations of neurosis can be valuable, he himself favored the energic or final viewpoint and

---

[27] Ibid., par. 6.
[28] "The Theory of Psychoanalysis," *Freud and Psychoanalyis,* CW 4, pars. 254f.

considered it indispensable to any theory of psychological development. The causal view of regression, for instance, sees it determined by, say, a mother fixation. But from the final standpoint, writes Jung, "the libido regresses to the *imago* of the mother in order to find there the memory associations by means of which further development can take place."[29]

The difference between the personal mother and the "imago" of the mother is the difference between a complex and an archetypal image. Behind the complex—the accretion of emotional associations with one's personal mother—there is everything that has ever been associated with "mother," positive and negative, in the history of mankind; that is the archetype of mother. Thus the regressed energy activates not only personal memories but archetypal images or symbols of "mother" that may never have been personally experienced.

Accordingly, Jung stresses that "what to the causal view is *fact* to the final view is *symbol,* and vice versa. Everything that is real and essential to the one is unreal and inessential to the other."[30]

An exclusively causal view of neurosis, notes Jung, may actually inhibit development, since it binds one's energy to the past and to elementary facts (for instance, to childhood and the personal mother). The final view, on the other hand, encourages development by transforming causes into means to an end, "into symbolic expressions for the way that lies ahead":

> Psychic development cannot be accomplished by intention and will alone; it needs the attraction of the symbol, whose value quantum [i.e., the energy invested in it] exceeds that of the cause. But the formation of a symbol cannot take place until the mind has dwelt long enough on the elementary facts, that is to say until the inner or outer necessities of the life-process have brought about a transformation of energy.[31]

The transformation of energy in this way is central to Jung's idea of what happens in neurosis. It involves both the principle of equivalence, as mentioned, and the principle of entropy, according to which the transformation of energy in a closed system is only possible as a result of

---

[29] "On Psychic Energy," *The Structure and Dynamics of the Psyche,* CW 8, par. 43.

[30] Ibid., par. 45.

[31] Ibid., par. 47.

differences in the intensity of energy that exists between different elements in that system.

Mix hot water with cold and you end up with water that is warm. The transfer of energy from one to the other leads to an equalization of differences. Within the system there is a transformation; it has balanced itself. Jung applied this principle to the psyche, with specific reference to what occurs in a conflict situation:

> We can see this process at work in the development of a lasting and relatively unchanging attitude. After violent oscillations at the beginning the opposites equalize one another, and gradually a new attitude develops, the final stability of which is the greater in proportion to the magnitude of the initial differences. The greater the tension between the pairs of opposites, the greater will be the energy that comes from them. . . .
>
> Daily psychological experience affords proof of this . . . . The most intense conflicts, if overcome, leave behind a sense of security and calm which is not easily disturbed, or else a brokenness that can hardly be healed. Conversely, it is just these intense conflicts and their conflagration which are needed in order to produce valuable and lasting results.[32]

Jung compared the flow of psychic energy to a river: "The libido has, as it were, a natural penchant: it is like water, which must have a gradient if it is to flow."[33] This is an eminently practical consideration in a psychological crisis, where the energy flow is blocked. The problem in any particular case is to find the appropriate gradient. Here it is not a matter of will power, of rationally choosing an object or direction toward which the energy "ought" to flow. Want to make a commitment, a decision, for all the right reasons but your energy doesn't? Forget it. The question, again, is where does *it,* your energy, naturally want to go?

> What is it, at this moment and in this individual, that represents the natural urge of life? That is the question.[34]

This regularly raises a moral dilemma or heightens an already existing conflict. And that is precisely what is required, for it brings to light psychic contents that have been repressed.

---

[32] Ibid., pars. 49f.
[33] *Symbols of Transformation,* CW 5, par. 337.
[34] *Two Essays,* CW 7, par. 487.

I read on, flipping pages, following threads of thought. Is there a link, I wondered, between adaptation, energy and neurosis?

Jung says there is. He points out that the process of development from child to adult entails an increasing adaptation to the external world. Whenever a person's libido, in the process of adaptation, meets an obstacle, there is an accumulation of energy that normally gives rise to an increased effort to overcome the obstacle. But if the obstacle seems to be insurmountable and the individual abandons the task of overcoming it, the stored-up energy regresses; it reverts to an earlier mode of adaptation. This in turn, writes Jung, activates infantile fantasies and wishes:

> The best examples of such regressions are found in hysterical cases where a disappointment in love or marriage has precipitated a neurosis. There we find those well-known digestive disorders, loss of appetite, dyspeptic symptoms of all sorts, etc. . . . [typically accompanied by] a regressive revival of reminiscences from the distant past. We then find a reactivation of the parental imagos, of the Oedipus complex. Here the events of early infancy—never before important—suddenly become so. They have been regressively reactivated. Remove the obstacle from the path of life and this whole system of infantile fantasies at once breaks down and becomes as inactive and ineffective as before.[35]

For these reasons, Jung declared that he did not seek the cause of a neurosis in the past, but in the present: "I ask, what is the necessary task which the patient will not accomplish?"[36] In terms of the developmental process, "the psychological trouble in neurosis, and the neurosis itself, can be formulated as *an act of adaptation that has failed.*"[37]

This is quite different from the classical Freudian view of neurosis, but it doesn't substantially change what happens in the process of analysis. The fantasies still have to be brought to light because the energy the person needs for psychic health—and for adaptation—is attached to them. The object in a Jungian analysis, however, is not to reveal a supposed root cause of the neurosis but to establish a connection between the conscious mind and the unconscious. Only in this way, believed Jung, can

---

[35] "Psychoanalysis and Neurosis," *Freud and Psychoanalysis,* CW4, par. 569.
[36] Ibid., par. 570.
[37] Ibid., par. 574.

the split-off energy become available for the accomplishment of the "necessary task" the person balks at. He says:

> Considered from this standpoint, psychoanalysis no longer appears as a mere reduction of the individual to primitive sexual wishes, but, if rightly understood, as a highly moral task of immense educational value.[38]

Jung's view of neurosis as an attempt at self-cure, and his application of the theory of conservation of energy to psychological phenomena, are cornerstones in the practice of analytical psychology. When one is depressed, for instance, a basic assumption is that the energy not available to consciousness has not simply vanished, but is busily stirring up unconscious contents that for the sake of psychological health need to be brought to light and examined. Thus, while a well-meaning friend might counsel distraction—"Get out more, mix with others, stop thinking about yourself" —the analyst sees the depression, or indeed any mood, as a challenge to find out what is going on inside. Hence one is encouraged to introspect, to stay with the mood—go into it rather than try to escape it.

In the normal course of life there is a relatively easy progression of energy, which is to say it can be directed more or less at will. "Progression," writes Jung, "could be defined as the daily advance of the process of psychological adaptation."[39] (This is not the same as development; progression refers simply to the continuous flow or current of life.)

In order to satisfy the demands of adaptation it is necessary to adopt or attain an attitude appropriate to given circumstances. As long as circumstances don't change, there is no reason to change one's attitude. But since circumstances do change, suddenly or over time, there is no one attitude that is permanently suitable.

Any change in the environment demands a new adaptation, which in turn requires a change in the attitude that was previously quite adequate. But a suitable attitude—that is, one that works in a given situation—is invariably characterized by a certain one-sidedness and is therefore resistant to change. When an attitude is no longer appropriate for the external situation, says Jung, the stage is set for neurosis:

---

[38] Ibid., par. 575.

[39] "On Psychic Energy," *The Structure and Dynamics of the Psyche,* CW 8, par. 60.

For example, a feeling-attitude that seeks to fulfil the demands of reality by means of empathy may easily encounter a situation that can only be solved through thinking. In this case the feeling-attitude breaks down and the progression of libido ceases. The vital feeling that was present before disappears, and in its place the psychic value of certain conscious contents increases in an unpleasant way; subjective contents and reactions press to the fore and the situation becomes full of affect and ripe for explosions.[40]

Such symptoms indicate a damming up of energy, marked by the breaking up of pairs of opposites.

During the progression of libido the pairs of opposites are united in the co-ordinated flow of psychic processes. . . . But in the stoppage of libido that occurs when progression has become impossible, positive and negative can no longer unite in co-ordinated action, because both have attained an equal value which keeps the scales balanced.   . . . The tension leads to conflict, the conflict leads to attempts at mutual repression, and if one of the opposing forces is successfully repressed a dissociation ensues, a splitting of the personality, or disunion with oneself.[41]

The struggle between the opposites would continue indefinitely if the process of regression—the backward movement of energy—did not set in with the outbreak of the conflict.

Through their collision the opposites are gradually deprived of value and depotentiated. . . . In proportion to the decrease in value of the conscious opposites there is an increase in value of all those psychic processes which are not concerned with outward adaptation and therefore are seldom or never employed consciously.[42]

As the energic value of these previously unconscious psychic processes increases, they manifest indirectly as disturbances in behavior, for example in what Freud called symptomatic actions and in the litany of emotional symptoms characteristic of neurosis.

Jung's view is that since the stoppage of libido is due to a failure of the dominant conscious attitude, the unconscious contents activated by regression contain the seeds of a new progression. In terms of his model of typology, the unconscious contents include the opposite attitude

---

[40] Ibid., par. 61.
[41] Ibid.
[42] Ibid., par. 62.

which, with the inferior functions, is potentially capable of complementing or even of replacing the inadequate conscious attitude.

> If thinking fails as the adapted function, because it is dealing with a situation to which one can adapt only by feeling, then the unconscious material activated by regression will contain the missing feeling function, although still in embryonic form, archaic and undeveloped. Similarly, in the opposite type, regression would activate a thinking function that would effectively compensate the inadequate feeling.[43]

The regression of energy thus confronts one with the problem of one's own psychology, as opposed to the initial difficulty of adapting to outer circumstances. In Jung's words, "regression leads to the necessity of adapting to the inner world of the psyche."[44] Prominent aspects of oneself that one needs to become aware of in such a situation are the persona (the "I" one presents to the outer world), the inner contrasexual (anima or animus) and the shadow (attitudes and inclinations that have either been repressed or never been conscious).

Looked at in this way, the regression of energy is not an abnormal symptom but quite as necessary a phase in the developmental process as is progression.

It seemed to me from all this that the progression of energy—that is, adaptation to outer conditions—was conceptually analogous to extraversion, and regression—requiring adaptation to inner conditions—was comparable to introversion. But according to Jung this is not the case:

> Progression is a forwards movement of life in the same sense that time moves forwards. This movement can occur in two different forms: either extraverted, when the progression is predominantly influenced by objects and environmental conditions, or introverted, when it has to adapt itself to the conditions of the ego (or, more accurately, of the "subjective factor"). Similarly, regression can proceed along two lines: either as a retreat from the outside world (introversion), or as a flight into extravagant experience of the outside world (extraversion). Failure in the first case drives a man into a state of dull brooding, and in the second case into leading the life of a wastrel.[45]

---

[43] Ibid., par. 65.
[44] Ibid., par. 66.
[45] Ibid., par. 77.

Well, it was now apparent to me the extent to which Jung's view of neurosis as an attempt at self-cure was based on the belief that the psyche is a self-regulating system. And it isn't only theory; it accords with the general experience that in a conflict situation, say, advice and suggestion have no lasting effect.

"A real solution," writes Jung, "comes only from within, and then only because the patient has been brought to a different attitude."[46] The conflict, he says, must be solved on a level of character where the opposites are taken sufficiently into account, "and this again is possible only through a change of character. . . . In such cases external solutions are worse than none at all."[47]

I had it all down pat and felt ready for Adam. I brandished the turnip like a sword and came down on his wrinkled old cabbage head with the wrath of God.

"Take that, you imp, you elf! And that, and that!"

I was beating him to a pulp when I woke up sobbing.

"There, there," soothed Adam. "It's okay. It's not me."

"Oh, cripes," I moaned. "Who are you?"

Adam shrugged. "Who am I, or who are you?"

"I don't know," I confessed.

"Let me ask you," said Adam, "is music composed of notes, or the spaces between?"

"I don't know."

"Why does water run instead of walk?"

"I don't know."

"Would stars twinkle with no eyes to see them?"

"Search me."

"Why do sneezes come in threes?"

I broke down.

"There seems to be a lot you don't know," said Adam. "There are things in your head that are not in your heart."

I had an inkling of what he meant.

---

[46] "Some Crucial Points in Psychoanalysis," *Freud and Psychoanalysis,* CW 4, par. 606.
[47] Ibid., par. 607.

"You need a holiday," he said. "Take a break. You are welcome to use my cottage."[48]

"But it's not winterized . . ."

"See for yourself," said Adam. "I believe you'll find it has all the comforts of home."

---

[48] Adam's summer home on Manitoulin Island in northern Ontario was the setting for my book *Who Am I, Really? Personality, Soul and Individuation.*

7
Typologically Speaking

It was three weeks before I could take Adam up on his offer. First there was Christmas and then the New Year. I like almost nothing about the Christmas season. Noise and bright lights, crowded streets, commercial hype, false cheer. It is a time when family complexes come out of the woodwork and I am busy holding hands. Worst of all, the post office is closed for two very long weekends.

However, I manage a good face and I do buy a tree. On Christmas Eve Rachel and J.K. come for dinner. I help J.K. decorate the tree; we open a present each, then we eat, open the rest of the presents and play games, in that order. That has been our tradition.

This year, when it came time for games and we were lolling in the living room enveloped by Christmas carols, J.K. said she was bored with Monopoly, Uno, Sorry and all the rest.

"Let's talk," she said. "We don't talk enough."

"That's because you're not around enough to talk to," said Rachel pointedly. They had been close for years. Now J.K. was fifteen and spent most of her out-of-school time with friends. Rachel missed their cozy bedtime chats, sharing the day; she had exciting things in her own life, but still, losing her daughter was not easy.

"What would you like to talk about?" I asked.

"Other people," said J.K. "I don't understand them."

"What don't you understand?"

"Well, like, they're so weird."

"Like how weird, what?"

"They say and do things I never would."

"Maybe to them, *you're* weird," I said. "Not everyone sees things the same way. Lalu isn't like you, is she?" Lalu was her best friend.

"No . . .," said J.K. Her long hair was purple this week; one side braided, the other spiked. Three silver rings hung from her left ear lobe. Her right arm sported a friendly dragon tattoo. She wore hard-top work boots over gray wool socks. Her tee-shirt was skimpy and brazen—

**I suffer from
P.M.S.
Putting Up With Men's Shit**

—her jeans fashionably faded and torn. Tall and slim, a goddess to my eyes; somebody's Winona, for sure.

I said, "What's Lalu good at?"

"Uh, gymnastics . . . ballet," said J.K.

"You're a whiz at math and your feets too big. What else?"

"Well . . . she likes to wear skirts and sneakers . . . and she's crazy about pistachios. I don't like any nuts."

"There you are," I said. "Just as people have different likes and dislikes, they function in different ways. That's called typology."

Rachel put in: "I used to work for a company that didn't hire anyone without giving them a type test."

J.K. looked from Rachel to me.

I sniffed. I'm pretty skeptical about type tests.[49] They are said to be useful in the business world so that square pegs don't get put into round holes; perhaps, but in terms of understanding yourself there is no substitute for prolonged self-reflection.

"Everyone has strengths and weaknesses," I said to J.K. "Right?"

"I guess," she said.

"Well, Jung suggested a way, a model, to put these into some order— how to understand the different ways in which people see the world."

I didn't need to tell J.K. who Jung was. She knows what I do for a living and I've used her artwork on the covers of some of my books. I think she's proud of that. So the books aren't at the top of her reading list; the covers are on her wall, aren't they? Right beside plastic mice, a pair of hand-cuffs, old license plates and a poster of a baby seal that says **Save the Animals, You're One Too.**

"If you realize that somebody is functioning in a particular way," I said, "you can make allowances. If you know how you yourself are liable to see things, you can compensate—maybe, in a particular situation, a different way would be more appropriate."

---

[49] See my *Personality Types: Jung's Model of Typology,* pp. 92ff.

"I know compensate," said J.K. "It means to make up for."

"Exactly," I said. "Jung used it to describe the process by which the psyche balances itself."

"Dad, can you be more specific?"

"Your psyche is all of you, consciousness and the unconscious too—everything you know about yourself and all the things you don't."

J.K. hunkered down by the tree and examined her favorite present, a fully manual camera with flash attachment and separate telephoto and wide angle lenses.

"Is typology a way of labeling people?" she asked.

"No," I said. "In fact Jung warned against that. He thought of his model as a tool for psychological orientation, to give direction—like using a compass when you're in the woods or go out canoeing."

J.K. said nothing. She was leafing through the camera manual and I thought she'd lost interest. I didn't mind. Photography was her current love; that's where her energy naturally went. But Rachel was there too; she seemed attentive. I should say that Rachel and I seldom talk psychology. She's read some Jung, of course, but there are many things we'd rather do when we're together than talk my shop.

Anyway, there we were this Christmas Eve, and the teacher came over me. I grabbed a pad and pencil and did a quick sketch.

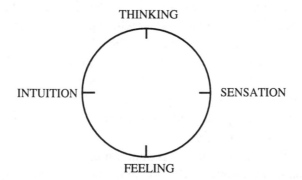

"This is Jung's basic model," I said. "There are four ways of functioning—thinking, feeling, intuition and sensation. Thinking and feeling are opposites, and so are intuition and sensation. Then there's introversion and extraversion—each of the four functions can work in an introverted or an extraverted way. You can turn the circle any way you like. I just arbitrarily put thinking at the top; any of the others might be there, depending on which function a person favors most."

"Don't go too fast," said Rachel, glancing at J.K.

"The sensation function," I said, "is concerned with tangible reality, the physical senses; it establishes that something exists. Thinking tells us what it is. Feeling tells us what it's worth to us, and through intuition— Jung described intuition as perception via the unconscious—we have a sense of what can be done with it."

"Dad, that's too fast," said J.K. So, she was still with us.

I slowed down and said much the same thing differently. "The sensation function excels at details; it takes things in like a photographic plate. Intuition is more interested in possibilities. The thinking function is concerned with ideas, and the feeling function focuses on relationship."

I went to the bookcase and pulled out Jung's *Psychological Types*. I leafed through it to what I wanted:

> For complete orientation all four functions should contribute equally: thinking should facilitate cognition and judgment, feeling should tell us how and to what extent a thing is important or unimportant for us, sensation should convey concrete reality to us through seeing, hearing, tasting, etc., and intuition should enable us to divine the hidden possibilities in the background, since these too belong to the complete picture of a given situation.[50]

I closed the book. "The ideal is to have conscious access to the function appropriate for a particular situation."

"Wicked," said J.K.

Rachel asked: "Is that possible?"

"Theoretically," I said. "But in fact most of us develop one function at the expense of the others. That's called our primary or superior function."

"Superior . . . ," said J.K., "meaning better?"

"Not in this context. One function isn't any better than any other; your superior function is just the one you're most likely to use."

"What happens to the others?" asked J.K.

---

[50] *Psychological Types,* CW 6, par. 900.

"Well," I said, "they give you a hard time. They pop up unexpectedly; they get you from behind. Especially your inferior function, the one you're least good at. In Jung's model that's the one opposite to your superior function. A one-sided emphasis on thinking, for instance, is invariably accompanied by an inferiority of feeling, and a well-differentiated sensation function shuts out intuition. And vice versa, of course.

"A person's typology is often a contributing factor in a psychological crisis. Part of my own problem, for instance, was that I relied too much on thinking and neglected the other functions; they finally demanded attention. My breakdown was a golden opportunity, really, because there was a lot of energy tied up with those functions. Becoming aware of that brought me a new lease on life." I smiled at them. "And you two."

Rachel smiled back. J.K. rolled her eyes.

"You can have two good functions, can't you?" said Rachel.

"Yes," I said. "One of those that isn't opposite to the primary function is often quite well developed. For example, thinking goes well with sensation or intuition, and a superior sensation function can have feeling or thinking as a good secondary function."

I drew another sketch. "Then you have something that might look like this—intuition and thinking work together in the speculative thinker, thinking and sensation combine for empirical thinking, and so on."

They studied my drawing.

"How do you know what your best function is?" asked J.K. "And which one isn't?"

"It's not easy," I said.

I thought: Should I go deeper? Discuss how emotion distorts the way we function? That we can't think straight when we're angry? That we can't evaluate what something is worth to us when we're upset? That possibilities dry up when we're depressed? Should I say a word or two about complexes and the difference between affect and the feeling function? About how all the functions operate below par when we're complexed? And then there's projection . . .

"Hey there," waved J.K. She spoke urgently into her fist: "Earth to Dad, are you there? Come in please . . . buzoom buzoom, bsst, bsst . . . do you copy?" She jumped up and pointed her camera at me. "Smile! "

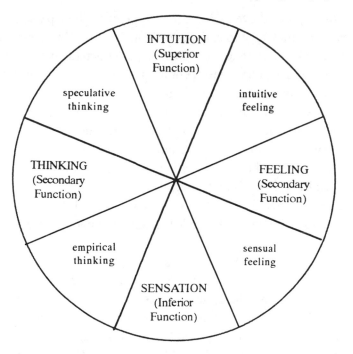

I swatted at her. She fell on the floor and clutched her head. "I am a majorly abused child," she moaned. "I am fat and ugly and nobody likes me. I shall sue the world for mega-damages."

Rachel grabbed her and they rolled around giggling. I took hold of my Christmas bugle and blew a few notes. Sunny surfaced from under a pile of wrapping paper and howled.

"Using Jung's model," I said finally, "is a matter of reflecting on what happens in your life. Ask yourself: In this situation, with that person, how did I function? With what effect? Did my actions and the way I expressed myself truly reflect my judgments—thinking and feeling—and my perceptions—sensation and intuition? To what end? Did I mess things up? What does that say about me? What can I do about it? What do I *want* to do about it? All that is called differentiation. Not everyone has a mind for it."

J.K. cradled her head in her hands and looked at me.

Rachel said: "Tell her more about introversion and extraversion."

"They are different ways of relating to the world," I said. "Introverts respond to people and events from the inside out. Their personal values are primary and they tend to resist outside influences. Extraverts are a lot more open and responsive to what goes on in the outside world; they love get-togethers and meeting new people. These two opposite types frequently fall in love, because one complements the other. Of course the opposite is also in ourselves, but it takes time and experience to realize that. In the meantime, we are prone to being fascinated by, or taking a dislike to, someone who seems to be unlike ourselves."

Shamefully simple, but it was Christmas Eve after all.

"Dad," said J.K., "is this stuff useful?"

"It has been to me," I said. "I was one-sided and I didn't know it. Now I understand myself better and I'm less likely to expect people to be what they aren't."

"So what type do you think I am?" she asked.

"I could hazard a guess," I said, "but I won't; that's for you to mull over. Anyway, I think the functions aren't yet differentiated in you; you're still a bowl of soup. Don't take that personally; most grown-ups are too. Look me up in twenty years. We'll talk about it."

J.K. gave me a big hug. "Merry Christmas, oh fatherly figure," she said, and bounced up the stairs with the latest rock video. Rachel helped me clear the table and stack the dishwasher. She got out her sketch book and was soon absorbed.

I plugged in a tape of Bach's flute sonatas and put my feet up. My mind went back to the time when Arnold and I were together in Zürich. I learned a good deal about typology from living with him. Theory is all very well. This was the horse's mouth.

Arnold and I were accepted into the training program at the same time. We hadn't known each other before, but when we met we hit it off. I was going to be in Zürich a week ahead so I offered to look for a place we could share. He thought that was a wonderful idea. I didn't know then that Arnold was a raving intuitive, or what was in store for me because of it. In those days my sensation function was tops; I tracked all the details.

I met Arnold at the station when he arrived. It was the third train I'd met. True to his type, his letter had not been specific; true to mine, I was.

"I've rented a house in the country," I told him, hefting his bag. The lock was broken and the straps were gone. One wheel was missing. "Twelve and a half minutes on the train and it's never late. The house has green shutters and paisley wallpaper. The landlady says we can furnish it the way we want."

"That's great," said Arnold, holding a newspaper over his head—*The International Herald Tribune* it was, October 6, 1974. It was pouring. He had no hat and no raincoat. He was wearing slippers, for God's sake. We couldn't find his trunk because he'd booked it through to Lucerne.

"Lucerne, Zürich," he said philosophically, "it's all Switzerland to me."

It was quite amusing at first. I'd never been that close to anyone quite so . . . well, different..

Time meant nothing to Arnold. He missed trains, he missed appointments. He was invariably late for lectures and if he finally found the right room he didn't have anything to write with. He either had bags of money or none at all. He didn't know east from west; he got lost whenever he left the house, and sometimes in it.

"You need a seeing-eye dog," I joked.

"Not with you around," he grinned.

He left the stove on overnight. He never turned out lights. Pots boiled over, meat turned black, while he sat on the porch watching the sky. The kitchen was forever filled with the smell of burnt toast. He lost his keys, his wallet, his lecture notes, his passport. He never had a clean shirt. In his scruffy old leather jacket, baggy jeans and sockless shoes he looked like a bum. His room was always a mess, like a hurricane had hit.

"It drives me crazy just to look at you," I would hum, adjusting my tie in the mirror.

I liked to be neatly turned out; it made me feel good. I knew precisely where everything was. My desk was ordered, my room just so. I made my bed and hung up my clothes. I turned out the lights when I left the house and I had an excellent sense of direction. I was always on time and I didn't lose anything. I could cook and I could sew. I knew exactly how much money was in my pocket. I never forgot a thing.

"You don't live in the real world," I observed, as Arnold set out to fry an egg. A real hero's journey. He couldn't find the frying pan and when he did he put it on the wrong burner. He broke the egg and yolk dribbled down his sleeve.

"Reality as *you* know it," he said, making a face. "Damn!" He'd burnt himself again.

I need not say much about the aggravations due to Arnold being an extravert and me considerably less so. Enough to say there were plenty. He brought strange people home at all hours of the day and night. I liked privacy, my own quiet space. During the day I escaped to my room; at night I lay in bed with a pillow over my head, trying not to listen. On occasion I'd catch a whiff of perfume, a giggle. I shooed them all away; I had a study timetable to keep and carousing wasn't on it.

On the other hand, Arnold's way of functioning was sometimes quite helpful. Like when we furnished the house.

Our landlady, Gretchen, was a trim and efficient businesswoman. She immediately took a fancy to Arnold. God knows why, he didn't present as well as I did. Her directions were generous.

"Just pick out what you want," she said. "You do the shopping, I'll pay the bills."

I had a few things in mind. So did Arnold. My ideas were quite modest; Arnold's were not. We already had beds and a few chairs. "A nice comfortable sofa," I said, as we entered the department store. "A bookcase and a desk for each of us, a couple of lamps. That's all we need."

"You have no imagination," said Arnold, steering me to the antiques. "You do the talking."

Naturally. I had not come to Zürich without learning German. Before leaving Toronto I took a Berlitz course for six months. I wasn't fluent but I could make myself understood. I could also get by in French and Italian. Arnold couldn't even count in any language but English. I believe he did not realize he was coming to a foreign country. I scolded him about this more than once.

"A few phrases," I implored. "Try saying hello, *Guten Tag*. Goo-ten Tak. Or please and thank you, *Bitte, Danke,* Bitt-ah, Dank-ah."

He shrugged. "They all speak English."

As it turned out, they didn't. Worse, and to my chagrin, the language of the streets was Swiss German, a dialect almost as different from

German as Welsh is from English. I was just about as helpless as Arnold.

Back to the department store. In one language or another we managed to spend a lot of our landlady's money. While I fumbled to say exactly what I meant, Arnold spoke in tongues; he waved his hands and jumped about; he pointed and drew pictures in the air. By the time we left, ushered out by a grateful crowd of salespeople who were now undying friends, we'd bought a few things I hadn't thought of, like a Chinese decorated screen, two Indian carpets, a complete set of Wedgewood dishes, eight pounds of bratwurst and numbered prints by Miro, Braque and Chagall. It would all be delivered.

Gretchen was thrilled. She invited us to her place for a special dinner and served a rare local wine she said didn't travel. She gave us a tape of the Swiss flutist Peter-Lukas Graf, which I still have.

Arnold stayed behind when I left. "I'll just wrap up the lease," he said.

I struggled to appreciate Arnold. I wanted to. His outgoing nature, his natural ebullience, were charming. I admired his air of careless confidence. He was the life of every party. He easily adapted to new situations. He was adventurous and lively. Everywhere he went he made friends. And then brought them home.

Arnold had an uncanny sense of perception. Whenever I got in a rut, bogged down in routine, he had something new to suggest. His mind was fertile; it seethed with plans and new ideas. His hunches were off the wall but often right. It was like he had a sixth sense. My own vision was totally mundane; where I saw a thing or a person, Arnold saw soul.

But problems constantly arose between us. When he expressed an intention to do something I took him at his word. I believed he would do what he said he would, and often he didn't. This was particularly annoying when we would arrange to meet at a certain time and place and he did not show up.

"Look," I said once when I finally caught him on the fly, "I counted on you. I bought the tickets, I held your seat. Where were you?"

"I got waylaid," he grinned.

I blew up.

"You're unstable," I fumed. "I can't depend on you. You're irresponsible and you're flighty. You are the quintessential puer. Why, you don't have a standpoint at all.' '

That wasn't how Arnold saw it.

"I think in terms of possibilities," he said. "They aren't real until I give them a voice and when I do they take on shape. But that doesn't mean I'm committed to them. Something more interesting might turn up. I don't feel tied to what I say. I can't help it if you take everything so literally."

He went on: "I have birds in my head. They come and they go. Sometimes I go with them, sometimes not. I never know in advance; it takes time to authenticate their flight."

One morning I got up to find yet another pot boiled empty on a hot burner. Arnold struggled out of bed, looking for his glasses.

"Have you seen my razor?" he called.

"God damn it!" I shouted, furious, grabbing an oven mitt. "One day you'll burn down the house; we'll both be cinders. 'Alas,' they'll say, scooping our remains into little jars to send back to our loved ones, 'they had such potential. Too bad one of them was such a klutz!' "

Arnold shuffled into the kitchen as I threw the pot out the door.

"Oh yeah?" he said. "You made dinner last night for Cynthia, I believe. I wasn't even here."

It was true. My face reddened. My balloon was pricked. Reality as I knew it suddenly got bigger.

"I'm sorry," I said meekly. "I forgot."

Arnold clapped his hands and danced around the room.

"Join the human race!" he sang. As usual, he couldn't hold a tune.

It was not until then that I realized Arnold was my shadow. This was a revelation. It shouldn't have been—we had already established that our complexes were radically different—but it struck me like a thunderbolt. I said as much to Arnold.

"Never mind," he grinned. "You're mine as well. That's why you drive me up the wall."

We embraced.

All that was a long time ago. Over the next few years I became more like Arnold, and he, in fact, more like me. He could finally tell left from right; he ironed his tee-shirts and he actually learned to crochet. He bought a computer and mastered it. He had a magnificent garden and he knew the names of all the flowers, in Latin even.

Meanwhile, I had raucous dinner parties and would often haunt the bars till dawn. I misplaced precious papers. I forgot names and telephone numbers. I could no longer find my way around a strange city. I pursued possibilities while things to do piled up. I had to hire a cleaning lady.

Arnold and I led separate lives, but we saw each other from time to time. We were still shadow brothers, but the tables were somewhat turned.

I would tell him about my latest escapade. He'd shake his head.

"You damned gadabout," he'd say, punching my shoulder.

Arnold would show me his latest creation in clay or wood and describe quiet evenings by the fire with a few intimate friends. He said he never wanted to travel again. This from a man who used to be off and running on a whim.

"You're dull and predictable," I'd say, cuffing him.

When Arnold died a few years ago I was bereft. Without him out there I reverted to the way I'd been. But not, thankfully, all the way, because by then I had him inside. Move over Rachel, I said, make room for my friend, and she did.

8
Back to Manitoulin

Early in January I was on my way north with Sunny, a box of books and my Macintosh PowerBook. It was a seven-hour trip with stops, but the time flew. I had a grab-bag of favorite tapes—Barbra Streisand, Phoebe Snow, Miles Davis, flute concertos, Elton John, etc., etc.—and the radio, with news every half-hour and talk-shows that would of course pay for my call except, they were sorry, from a cell phone. There was a light snowfall but the road was clear, with little traffic.

On Manitoulin Island it was slower going. There were high drifts. The main roads had been plowed, but the laneway to Adam's cottage was completely blocked. I parked as close as I could get and made several trips on snowshoes to unload the car. Sunny struggled along beside through breast-high snow.

The cottage was as cold as the proverbial witch's tit. The water system was shut down, so the toilet didn't work. There were two space-heaters and a fireplace. I melted lake-ice. I found dry wood to make a fire and huddled by it under a blanket. Sunny curled around my feet. All the comforts of home, indeed. Whose comfort, whose home?

As I thawed I thought of my early teen-age years when my parents were dirt-poor. Home was a thin-walled cabin in a clutch of summer shacks. We had an outdoor privy and every morning, rain or shine, I trudged to the pump up the hill to fetch two pails of water, eyes peeled for Jill. I had a Mechano set and collected stamps. My mom cooked on an old iron wood-burning stove which also heated the house; one of my chores was to keep it fed. I had a dog named Smokey who was run over by a milk-truck; I cried for two days. My mother found a mouse in a toilet roll and screamed. I made a dollar fifty a week, plus tips, delivering papers; once I was set upon by a kennel of German Shepherds and Great Danes. I built model airplanes with my dad and I learned to ski.

My father was then a corporal in the Royal Canadian Air Force. He had joined up at the start of the Second World War. He didn't fire guns or bomb bridges; he worked in the payroll department. Before the war he had been a teller in a bank for two years and before that a brakeman on the Canadian National Railway. My mother had worked at the five and dime and was in a chorus line. They met at a church social when he was twenty years old and she was twenty-two. Theirs was an old-fashioned marriage: he brought the bacon home and while she cooked it he read the paper. Every day he told her he loved her; she got mad when he went out drinking after work instead of coming home for supper. I did my homework and the dishes. In the evening we listened to Amos 'n' Andy, Jack Benny and the Green Hornet. I don't remember having any problems.

My mother and father barely got through high school. They didn't begrudge my higher learning; they just didn't understand it. They knew nothing of their unlived lives, nor did I, for many years, of mine. Was I better than them for all that? Were their unexamined lives not worth living? Who was I to judge?

I dozed by the fire, wondering why, if I was answerable to no one, I continued to dig up questions.

In late afternoon I got down to business. I had been more than a little disturbed by my dream-beating of Adam. Where on earth did that come from? The same place, I suspected, as my reaction to his innocent remark in Mayday's[51]—my father complex. When I was in analysis I had become acutely aware of the ubiquitous influence of my mother complex, but I had barely looked at the role of the father; not willfully, it just had not come up. In Jungian analysis you don't stir a pot with nothing in it; you work on what you're immediately confronted with and bide your time for the rest; its turn will come, or not, and if not then it's not important. Now, it seemed, its turn had come; ergo, it must be important.

I hardly knew where to start. But then I realized where I was: Manitoulin = legendary home of the Ojibway Great Father, Kitche Manitou; island = a mass of land surrounded by water, the unconscious, split off from the ego-mainland; that is, a complex. So, I had already started.

Adam was closely associated in my mind with Jung. Consciously I had the highest regard for them both. Others might question their morals, their ideas, their judgment. Not me. I've been true blue. Maybe, in an ef-

---

[51] Above, p. 13.

fort at compensation, my self-regulating psyche was saying I've been too true, too blue; I've given them more than they're due.

On the other hand, maybe I hadn't given them *enough*. That's compensation too; the psyche can torpedo a conscious ego-attitude, or, just the opposite, support it. My head swam.

I resolved to follow up all the references to the father in Jung's Collected Works and see what happened. It might make another chapter; if it didn't work I could always scrap it. Nobody need know but me. And my Rachels, of course; I don't keep much from them.

I cast about for a narrative device. Sunny was handy.

"Come," I said.

She scrambled to her feet, ears perked.

"Sit," I said. She did.

I bowed my head. "We are gathered here in the land of Kitche Manitou to talk about Jungian psychology and me. Speak now if you know of any impediment to this project, or by your troth forever hold your peace."

I looked up. Sunny wagged her bushy tail.

"Okay, this is a game. You pretend you're you and I'll pretend I'm me. Don't worry, I'll do most of the talking. Okay?"

"Arf!" she said. "Arf! Arf!"

"Good girl," I said, and gave her a cookie. I put another log on the fire and poured myself a dram of Scotch. I find I function better in this mode when my mind is slightly askew. This is consistent with Jung's view that the inferior functions are more accessible during an *abaissement du niveau mentale*—when you're not your usual self. A joint used to do that for me, only rather too much; I completely forgot who I was. Now a little alcohol does the trick. Sometimes it also brings up Arnold.

He was suddenly there, plain as day.

"Arnold, you big oaf!" I ran to hug him.

"Where am I?" he said. He looked around.

"Last year," I prompted. "We were here with Adam and Rachel and J.K. And Norman too."[52]

---

[52] Norman, a former analysand of mine, was Adam's assistant, currently on a leave of absence. His story is the subject of my *Survival Papers: Anatomy of a Midlife Crisis*.

"Yeah, I remember this place," said Arnold. "Nice food and wine. That crazy old fart with the Chicken Little complex. What ever happened to him, anyway?"

I rejoiced. This was the old Arnold, scornful of any authority.

"Adam is doing his thing," I said. "Sunny, come, look who's here." Arnold was always one of her favorites. She came and sniffed.

"I have missed you," I said, and for an hour we reminisced about the things we'd done together, how it felt, what it all meant. I loved Arnold; I wouldn't be who I was without him.

"Enough of this sloppy sentiment," said Arnold at last. "What are you up to now?"

"Well, I have a book on the go. At this very moment I'm working on the father. Sunny has agreed to help. Want to join us?"

Arnold grinned, wide as ever. "I'm game."

"Arf!" said Sunny. She licked him up and down.

I rubbed my hands. First I was one, then I was two, now I was three. Could the fourth be far behind?[53]

I stoked the fire.

"As you know," I said to my cohorts, "Jung's comments on the father complex were rarely more than asides in writing about something else. About all he says specifically, in terms of men, is that in general the complex manifests itself in the persona, through identification with the personal father, and as aspects of a man's shadow, through introjection. In a woman it manifests in the nature of the animus, considerably colored by the projection of her father's anima.[54] However, at the core of the father complex is the archetype of the father, and Jung had quite a lot to say about that. On your mark now, let's go."

For the next few hours we pored through the Collected Works, tagging pages with yellow stickies. Surrounded by open books, sharing a bottle, it

---

[53] I was thinking of the alchemical Axiom of Maria: "One becomes two, two becomes three, and out of the third comes the one as the fourth." Jung saw this as a metaphor for the process of individuation: *one* is the original state of unconscious wholeness; *two* signifies the conflict between opposites; *three* points to a potential resolution; *the third* is the transcendent function; and *the one as the fourth* is a transformed state of consciousness, relatively whole and at peace.

[54] See "The Syzygy: Anima and Animus," *Aion,* CW 9ii, pars. 20ff.

was just like old times. In the weeks leading up to our Diploma exams we had many such sessions. Arnold used to say he depended on me to do the thinking. In turn, I could not have done without his intuitive ability to connect disparate thoughts. Much as Jung himself, actually.

For instance, in his essay on the Trinity, Jung discusses the symbolism of Father, Son and Holy Ghost in terms of three stages in a psychological developmental process. "The world of the Father," he writes, "typifies an age which is characterized by a pristine oneness with the whole of Nature,"[55] an age far removed from critical judgment and moral conflict. It is humankind in its childhood state. It corresponds psychologically to unconsciousness. The second stage, the world of the Son, says Jung,

> is a world filled with longing for redemption and for that state of perfection in which man was still one with the Father. Longingly he [looks] back to the world of the Father, but it [is] lost forever, because an irreversible increase in man's consciousness had taken place in the meantime and made it independent.
>
> The stage of the "Son" is therefore a conflict situation *par excellence* . . . . "Freedom from the law" brings a sharpening of opposites.[56]

This state of affairs corresponds to the meaning of the number two, which symbolizes the conflict of opposites. The Holy Ghost takes Jung to the symbolism of the third stage in the developmental proces:

> The advance to the third stage means something like a recognition of the unconscious, if not actual subordination to it. . . . Just as the transition from the first stage to the second demands the sacrifice of childish dependence, so, at the transition to the third stage, an exclusive independence has to be relinquished.
>
> This third stage . . . means articulating one's ego-consciousness with a supraordinate totality, of which one cannot say that it is "I," but which is best visualized as a more comprehensive being.[57]

I read these gems to Arnold with great passion.

"Interesting," he said. "Now hear this":

---

[55] "A Psychological Approach to the Dogma of the Trinity," *Psychology and Religion,* CW 11, par. 201.
[56] Ibid., pars. 203, 272.
[57] Ibid., pars. 273, 276.

The father represents the world of moral commandments and prohibitions, although, for lack of information about conditions in prehistoric times, it remains an open question how far the first moral laws arose from dire necessity rather than from the family preoccupations of the tribal father. At all events it would be easier to keep one's eye on a boxful of spiders than on the females of a primal horde.[58]

"Jung compares women to spiders!" I hooted. "That will ruffle a few feathers. What else?"

Arnold read on:

The father is the representative of the spirit, whose function it is to oppose pure instinctuality. That is his archetypal role, which falls to him regardless of his personal qualities; hence he is very often an object of neurotic fears for the son. Accordingly, the monster to be overcome by the son frequently appears [in myth and legend] as a giant who guards the treasure.[59]

I said, "Like that awesome creature Humbaba who guarded the Great Mother Ishtar in the Gilgamesh epic. When Gilgamesh and his shadow-brother Enkidu bested Humbaba, Ishtar offered herself to Gilgamesh and he turned her down."

Arnold nodded, scanning the page. "Jung says that by refusing the mother the hero becomes equal to the sun; he renews himself. In the Mithraic tradition the killing of the bull has the same significance":

[The bull] represents the father who—paradoxically—enforces the incest prohibition as a giant and dangerous animal. The paradox lies in the fact that, like the mother who gives life and then takes it away again as the "terrible" or "devouring" mother, the father apparently lives a life of unbridled instinct and yet is the living embodiment of the law that thwarts instinct. There is, however, a subtle though important distinction to be made here: the father commits no incest, whereas the son has tendencies in that direction. The paternal law is directed against incest with all the violence and fury of uninhibited instinct. . . . But as the "father," the representative of moral law, is not only an objective fact, but a subjective factor in the son himself, killing the bull clearly denotes an overcoming of animal instinct.[60]

---

[58] *Symbols of Transformation,* CW 5, par. 396.
[59] Ibid.
[60] Ibid.

"So," I summarized, "the son-hero must overcome his animal nature in order to avoid incest with the mother, which would be to fall back into unconsciousness; he then takes over the role of the father and can do whatever he wants. The big round."

"I think you've got it," said Arnold dubiously.

"Animals represent instinct," I said patiently, "and also the opposite, the prohibition of instinct. Jung is saying that man becomes human through conquering his animal instinctuality. He can then use it in his life appropriately, instead of being used by it. For instance, he can direct his sexual energy toward one woman instead of it being available willy-nilly to the next Winona. I should think that would facilitate the possibility of a long-term relationship, wouldn't you?"

Arnold said nothing. Long-term relationships weren't exactly his strong suit. He leafed through another book to a yellow sticky. "What about this: 'Too much of the animal distorts the civilized man, too much civilization makes sick animals'?"[61]

"It fits," I said confidently, though I wasn't sure exactly how. "Ah, here is sheer poetry," and I read:

> The mother who gives warmth, protection, and nourishment is also the hearth, the sheltering cave or hut, and the surrounding vegetation. She is the provident field, and her son is the godlike grain, the brother and friend of man. She is the milk-giving cow and the herd. The father goes about, talks with other men, hunts, travels, makes war, lets his bad moods loose like thunderstorms, and at the behest of invisible thoughts he suddenly changes the whole situation . . . . He is the war and the weapon, the cause of all changes; he is the bull provoked to violence or prone to apathetic laziness. He is the image of all the helpful or harmful elemental powers.[62]

Sunny had meanwhile been nosing elsewhere. Now she pawed a page in *The Archetypes and the Collective Unconscious;* it was another gem:

> In men, a positive father-complex very often produces a certain credulity with regard to authority and a distinct willingness to bow down before all spiritual dogmas and values.[63]

---

61 "The Eros Theory," *Two Essays,* CW 7, par. 32.
62 "Mind and Earth," *Civilization in Transition,* CW 10, par. 67.
63 "The Phenomenology of the Spirit in Fairytales," CW 9i, par. 396.

"Oh, good girl!" I said.

"Arf!" said Sunny. She tore around the room a couple of times and then leaped onto the kitchen counter, where she stood panting.

"Bad girl!" I said, for she was not allowed on the furniture. What the hell, I threw her another cookie. She wolfed it down and smacked her lips. Then she found a voice.

"I am quite familiar with your problem," she said." I first came across it when investigating images in dreams. It struck me that a certain kind of father complex has a spiritual character, so to speak, in the sense that the father-image gives rise to statements, actions, tendencies, impulses, opinions and so on to which one can hardly deny the attribute 'spiritual.' "

Arnold stood and clapped. "Hey! How do you do it?"

I rubbed my eyes. "Not without difficulty." And I grabbed a pen.

"The archetype of the mother," said Sunny, "is the most immediate one for the child. But with the development of consciousness the father also enters one's field of vision, activating an archetype whose nature is in many respects opposed to that of the mother. Just as the mother archetype corresponds to the Chinese *yin,* so the father archetype corresponds to the *yang.* It determines our relations to the collective, to the law and the state, to reason and to the spirit. The father represents authority, hence also the law and the state. He is that which moves in the world, like the wind; the guide and creator of invisible thoughts and airy images.

"At first he is *the* father, an all-encompassing God-image, a dynamic principle. In the course of life this authoritarian imago recedes into the background: the father turns into a limited and often all-too-human personality. The father-image, however, develops to the full its potential significance. The place of the personal father is taken by the society of men, and the place of the mother by the family."

Arnold whispered: "You could take her on the lecture circuit."

"You mean you could," I said.

"In dreams and visions," continued Sunny, "it is always a father-figure from whom the decisive convictions, prohibitions and wise counsels emanate. Frequently it consists simply of an invisible but authoritative voice, though for the most part the spiritual factor is symbolized by the figure of a wise old man who appears in the guise of a magician, doctor, priest, professor or the like. Sometimes the part is played by a real spirit, namely the ghost of someone dead, or, more rarely, by gnome-like figures, dwarfs, elves or, rarest of all, talking animals."

Arnold guffawed.

"The spirit-figure can be positive," said Sunny, "signifying the higher personality or Self. But it can also be negative, and then it signifies the infantile shadow."

I looked up from writing. "How can we tell the difference?"

Sunny lay on the counter with her front paws over the edge.

"Unfortunately," she said, "it can never be established with any certainty whether these spirit-figures are morally good. Often they show all the signs of duplicity, if not outright malice."

She bared her sharp white teeth and slavered. Instantly I was thirteen and struggling to get out from under a pack of snarling beasts. I shook my head. It was only Sunny.

"I must emphasize, however," she said, "that the grand plan on which the unconscious life of the psyche is constructed is so inaccessible to our understanding that we can never know what evil may not be necessary in order to produce good by enantiodromia, and what good may very possibly lead to evil. Often it is a matter of having patience, of wait and see. If you go far enough in one direction, you know, anything can turn into its opposite. Saul's conversion on the road to Damascus; it happens."

"Amen," nodded Arnold. His own brother had been a fire and brimstone tent-preacher who became a professional wrestler after a drunken week in a brothel.

Sunny got up and paced her narrow perch.

"The archetype of spirit," she said, "in one shape or another, generally appears in a situation where insight, understanding, good advice, determination, planning, etcetera, are needed but cannot be mustered on one's own resources. The archetype compensates this state of spiritual deficiency by contents designed to fill the gap. In fairy tales, for instance, an old man or a helpful animal appears when the hero is in a hopeless and desperate situation from which only profound reflection or a lucky idea—in other words, a spiritual function or an endopsychic automatism

of some kind—can extricate him. But since, for internal or external reasons, the hero cannot accomplish this himself, the knowledge needed to
compensate the deficiency comes in the form of personified thoughts."

"An endopsychic automatism . . .," marveled Arnold.

"What is my gap?" I asked, all ears and a few tears.

"There!" said Sunny, pointing her snout at Arnold. "Did you hear
that? He wants the answer on a plate. It is hard to know whether that
comes from a positive mother complex or from having a father who
never asked the question."

"My dad was a simple man," I protested. "Good was good. He knew
no better." But just then I remembered coming home with a cut or a
scrape; my dad would examine it and shake his head, "Doesn't look
good, son—but better than a kick in the head by a horse." Did that count?

Arnold jerked a thumb at me and said to Sunny: "He once told me his
fantasy of a Big Book that contained all the solutions to all the conflicts
one could ever have. When you were up against it, why you'd just go to
the General Index."

I daggered him a look. That had been a drunken confidence.

"Sunny," I pleaded, "I am listening."

"I cannot fill your gap," she said, "but I can give you an example of
compensation. It is a dream I had as a pup. As it happens, it is quite similar to one Jung recounts,[64] which just goes to show that archetypal motifs
know no boundaries.

"My master at that time was a young theological student with a good
heart and a hair shirt. He had dedicated himself to Jesus and had no
knowledge of what we would call his shadow. From his spartan cell he
had a view of a room in which a lady of the night entertained her callers.
Before long he found himself with what he had been taught were impure
thoughts. He prayed and confessed them but they did not go away. He
beat himself with hickory sticks but they persisted.

"Finally he dreamed. Or rather I did. We were very close, you see; my
dream was his. And it was this:

"He was standing in the presence of a sublime old man identified as

---

[64] Ibid., par. 398.

the white magician, though he was wearing a long black robe. He had just ended a lengthy discourse with the words: 'And for that we need the help of the black magician.' Then the door opened and another old man came in. This was the black magician, who was however dressed in a white robe. He too looked noble and sublime. He evidently wanted to speak with the white magician, but hesitated to do so in the presence of the dreamer. 'Speak,' said the white magician, 'he is an innocent.'

"So the black magician proceeded to tell a strange story of his adventures in finding the lost keys of Paradise; now he had them but did not know how to use them. He had come to the white magician, he said, to learn the secret of the keys.

"I woke up refreshed and so did the student. He subsequently became a much-loved parish priest who took sinful transgressions with a grain of salt; for himself he took a mistress."

Sunny stopped and began to groom herself.

I glanced at Arnold. He shrugged.

"Well?" I said to Sunny.

"Well what?" she said. "White needs black and black needs white. The unconscious presented my master not with a simple solution to his dilemma, but rather with a way of looking at a problem we all come up against: the uncertainty of moral valuation, the bewildering interplay of good and evil, the remorseless concatenation of guilt, suffering and redemption. This is the traditional path to the primordial religious experience, but how many can recognize it? It is like a still small voice that sounds from afar. It is ambiguous, questionable, dark, presaging danger and hazardous adventure; a razor-edged path to be trod only for the sake of the soul, without assurance and without sanction."

My first thought was of my dream of a spider on skis, riding a razorblade. Then suddenly I recognized Sunny's voice. She was pretending to be Adam, paraphrasing Jung. My heart melted; greater love hath no dog. I tossed her two cookies.

So, in one fell swoop we were not four but five—the alchemical quintessence! The *filius regius,* the *unus mundus,* the Philosophers' Stone— mine, all mine! I flung myself into bed, warm at last.

9
Ojibway Vision

I awoke next morning feeling cold and hung over and very much alone. I had dreamed of taking my father to the film *A Star Is Born;* first I could not find a place to park the car, and when we finally got to the theater there were no seats left. Groan.

The fire had died; I laid another. After toast and porridge and a brisk romp with Sunny—not so easy in a blizzard and two feet of snow—I went back to the yellow stickies to see what I could salvage. I browsed aimlessly. Nothing made much sense. I'd lost the thread. Whatever had possessed me was gone.

"Sunny," I commanded, "speak!"

"Arf!" she said. "Arf!"

Dumb dog. I hugged her and gave her a cookie.

I put Jung aside and found a deck of cards. I played solitaire and blackjack and all four hands of bridge. I played computer games. I tossed cards into a hat, pennies against the wall. I kept losing. I thought of the poem J.K. wrote a couple of years ago. It began:

> why do things
> never seem
> quite to go my way
> not this
> not that
> not anything
> wants to go my way

I went through Adam's bookshelf. There were guides to trees and bats, flowers, birds, wildlife and mushrooms, cookbooks and novels: John Irving, Robertson Davies, Michener, Theodore Sturgeon, John Grisham and other potboilers. I opened *Up North: A Guide to Ontario's Wilderness from Blackflies to the Northern Lights.*

> Spiders are the very essence of "creepy" in the popular mind, the mere sight of one giving countless Miss Muffets the willies. Freud contended that spider phobias rise from a primal fear of a cannibal witch or ogre with

long, pointy, bending fingers, subconsciously identified with the arachnid's pointy, bending legs. The estimated weight of insects eaten annually by spiders in Canada is equal to the weight of the country's entire human population.[65]

There were books on Indian legends. I pulled out *Ojibway Heritage.* It fell open at a chapter headed "No Man Begins To Be Until He Has Received His Vision."[66] This phrase, according to the author, best expressed the Ojibway's fundamental understanding of a man's purpose in life.

Intrigued, I read on.

According to the Anishnabe, an Ojibway band in northern Ontario (including Manitoulin), man was a spontaneous being made out of nothing; that is, he was created from new substances unlike any of those out of which the physical world had been made.

> Out of corporeal and incorporeal substances was man created according to and in fulfilment of a vision of Kitche Manitou. Man was, in the abstract metaphysical sense, a composite being.
>
> But as the Anishnabe conceived man as a being endowed with a capacity for vision much like his creator, man became more than an abstract being, a creature of the mind. Man was bound to seek and fulfill vision and as such was a moral being.[67]

Only men were required "to seek and fulfill vision." (Women were free to do the same, but it was not an obligation; they were deemed to be complete already by virtue of having given birth to men.) Men also had to live out and give expression to their visions, for that is how they found purpose and gave meaning to their life and being. Each man was obligated to seek his purpose, according to his own capacity, not outside himself but within his innermost being. And because each was differently endowed, each attained a different vision and each fulfilled his vision as he understood it.

The vision a man received was a palpable force in his life. It could alter his conduct, mode of life and even his character. Moreover, with the

---

[65] Doug Bennet and Tim Tiner, *Up North,* p. 93.

[66] Basil Johnston, *Ojibway Heritage: The Ceremonies, Rituals, Songs, Dances, Prayers and Legends of the Ojibway,* p. 119.

[67] Ibid.

coming of vision, mere existence became living; that is, a man entered a moral order where his individual acts and conduct assumed a character and quality they did not previously posses. Prior to this he was, in a moral sense, incomplete, a half-being; on receiving his vision he gained purpose, which conferred meaning upon his actions and unity to his life.

> Purpose without quest is empty; a vision without fulfilment is vain. Just as Kitche Manitou received a vision and created matter, being, and life, so man in receiving a vision had to live it out.[68]

Besides fulfillment, vision required preparation. The capacity for vision, like other faculties, was only a potential capacity and its growth required nourishment. And because man was a composite being, his two substances needed preparation in order to attain the state of harmony necessary for the reception of the vision. Not until these corporeal and incorporeal substances were ready and worthy did the vision come. Not until a man was ready to live out the vision did he receive it.

In the Ojibway scheme of things, there were two dimensions to life; one was existence, the other a moral sense. The latter was by far the more significant. The physical dimension, because of the difficulty of survival, was considered to comprise four hills: infancy, youth, adulthood and old age. The moral dimension consisted of the preparation, the quest, the vision and the fulfillment, corresponding to the four physical phases.

> Though existence was hard, the vision had to be sought. There was no better way to achieve understanding of self and life. Moreover, it impressed merit upon a man and enabled him to endure the difficult life and to fulfil his purpose in life.[69]

In his twelfth year an Ojibway boy was deemed ready to begin his quest for vision. After purification ceremonies he was taken by his father to a remote, solitary place, unique by virtue of its mood and spirit. There the boy was left alone for four days to contemplate life, his being and existence. In solitude, his task was to bring his inner being and body into accord, at the same time conjoining with the earth and the animals and plants residing in the place of vision. He did not eat. His soul-spirit

---

[68] Ibid., p. 120.
[69] Ibid. pp. 120-121.

hunger had to be filled; his bodily hunger was more easily fed and could wait. In silence and peace would vision come, a gift to him who was prepared.

I remember once when I was about twelve, my father took me to a park where we sat by a pond and threw chunks of bread to swans. I became so absorbed I didn't notice him leave. When I realized I was alone I panicked. I ran about looking and was on the verge of tears when I saw him on his way back with ice-cream cones. Unprepared, I had envisioned only abandonment.

Ojibway boys who did not receive a vision continued the quest the following year, and the next and the next. For some the vision came early, inaugurating a new phase of being. For others it came late in life, and for some never.

There were three binding principles pertaining to visions:

1) Never interfere with the vision quest of another.

2) Never allow another to interfere in your quest.

3) Do not aspire to vision beyond your scope and ability.

Since vision was considered to be of a supernatural order and nature, and very personal, it demanded fulfillment. And while the general content and theme of a vision might be deduced from a person's subsequent conduct, recipients did not disclose their visions. The soul-spirit was inviolate and not to be shared.

The Anishnabe recognized three kinds of vision, the distinction being based on the way the vision came. One kind was received during the vigil. Its meaning was complete: it brought light and clarity, insight, self-understanding, sometimes suggesting one's destiny or career.

A second kind of vision was in the majority: it didn't come complete but in stages and under different circumstances, and often over a long period of time. Only after a number of such partial visions had been received would the entire meaning become clear.

The third kind was like the first, complete; it only differed in that it came during sleep, often rousing the dreamer to consciousness. Thus it was considered an "awakening."

In the physical order, vision was a dramatic revelation of purpose, character and sometimes avocation. In the moral order, vision was a birth, a becoming. According to the Anishnabe, from the moment of vision, a man began "to be," he was no longer a youth but an adult. At that moment, a man's acts and conduct assumed quality; purpose conferred character. Having received a vision, a man had then to live it out . . . a man had to be true to his vision.[70]

Well, needless to say I found all this pretty interesting, what with the specters of Arnold and Sunny fresh in my mind. But how was I to understand it psychologically? Was a man's vision simply a projection of what was in him to begin with? Did seeking it prevent neurosis? Did receiving it bring wholeness? Were there good visions and better ones?

Overall, it seemed to me that the Ojibway vision was comparable to a combination of what Jung referred to as "vocation" and "personality." I have written at length about these concepts elsewhere,[71] but a key passage by Jung is worth quoting here:

> What is it, in the end, that induces a man to go his own way and to rise out of unconscious identity with the mass as out of a swathing mist? Not necessity, for necessity comes to many, and they all take refuge in convention. Not moral decision, for nine times out of ten we decide for convention likewise. What is it, then, that inexorably tips the scales in favour of the *extra-ordinary?*
>
> It is what is commonly called *vocation:* an irrational factor that destines a man to emancipate himself from the herd and from its well-worn paths. True personality is always a vocation and puts its trust in it as in God, despite its being, as the ordinary man would say, only a personal feeling. But vocation acts like a law of God from which there is no escape. The fact that many a man who goes his own way ends in ruin means nothing to one who has a vocation. He *must* obey his own law, as if it were a daemon whispering to him of new and wonderful paths. Anyone with a vocation hears the voice of the inner man: he is *called.*[72]

For the Ojibway, living out one's vision was no less difficult than the quest. One made errors in judgment, or forgot. The Path of Life was portrayed on birch bark scrolls as tortuous—seven and sometimes nine branches digressed from the main road. Those straying from the main

---

[70] Ibid., p. 132.

[71] See *Who Am I, Really?*, pp. 52-71.

[72] "The Development of Personality," *The Development of Personality,* CW 17, pars. 299ff.

road were considered to have betrayed their vision. Such a state was tantamount to "non-living," a condition in which acts and conduct had no quality. To avoid such a state, men as well as women went on annual retreats to review their lives, to reflect on where they had strayed and how to resume the true path.

> Man in the last phase of life, old age, was considered to have acquired some wisdom by virtue of his living on and by fidelity to his vision. Wisdom was knowing and living out the principles of life as understood.[73]

Sunny and I stayed on for three more days. How did we spend the time? Staring at the wall, chipping ice, eating and sleeping, reading, keeping warm. By the time we left I felt renewed. I also knew at least one reason why I'd come: it was to free myself for a few days from the tyranny of the box—the post office box. Not much, but better than a kick in the head by a horse.

And Sunny, what did she did get out of it, besides a few extra cookies? Well, I won't put more words into her mouth. Maybe one day she'll tell me herself.

---

[73] Johnston, *Ojibway Heritage,* p. 133.

10
More on Complexes

Rachel and I went to visit Adam soon after my return from Manitoulin. A few days earlier I had given him my written account. Rachel had read it and said she wished she'd been there. I felt the same way. On the other hand, if she had been with me it would have been quite a different story. Roundabouts and swings; life in a nutshell.

Now Adam gave his assessment .

"I don't have much to say about vision quests," he said. "It is an interesting tradition, and archetypally sound as an initiation into adulthood. I understand that it is seldom practiced nowadays by the Ojibway themselves. Like many other native traditions it has been overwhelmed by the advance of civilization. For the most part it is kept alive by self-styled shamans leading package tours of misguided white folk."

I gulped.

Rachel said: "That's pretty harsh."

"It's pretty true," said Adam. "Vision quests are not in our blood. For most Westerners growing up is immensely more complicated. Our spiritual and intellectual heritage has spawned numerous discontents unknown to simpler cultures. Where ritual was good, consciousness is better. Come to that, visions are common enough without our having to seek them. I have had their like and I understand them, as Jung did, in terms of a momentary irruption of an unconscious content. The same thing happens in any mental disturbance.

"In any case, your experience of Arnold and Sunny was more of an active imagination than a vision, though I grant you there are similarities. You were troubled and did not know why. There were things you needed to become conscious of and you set out to discover them. I cannot fault your procedure. Tell me, why did you stop?"

"I . . . ran out of steam," I said.

"Steam . . .," mused Adam, "water, overheated . . . the unconscious on the boil . . . my dear fellow, is it possible that you were sidetracked by a complex?"

"I wouldn't be surprised," I said. "Which one?"

"Ah," said Adam, "a reasonable question."

He refilled our cups with tea from a copper samovar. We were snacking on a picnic lunch from the local deli: smoked salmon, Hungarian salami, pumpernickel bread, a light green salad. And Swedish caviar, of course.

"You have an irresistible desire to put names to things," he said. "I do too; it is the shadow side of a well-developed thinking function—or alternatively, symptomatic of an inferior one. By giving something a name we imagine we escape its effects. That is magical thinking. It is characteristic of the primitive mind, and it is certainly an illusion. The complexes go their merry way in spite of what we think. The only certainty is that they are out of our control."

I felt a lecture coming on and said, half-jokingly, "Adam, shall I get the turnip?"

He laughed. "You see? Now your sensation function wants in. It needs something to hold on to. Where is your feeling, your intuition? What is this worth to you? What are the possibilities?"

"I thought you were going to talk about complexes," I said, somewhat miffed.

"And I am," said Adam.

He got up and toured the studio, whistling. He fed the fauna and watered the flora. Everything else he looked intently at.

I glanced at Rachel. She seemed to be enjoying this. Well, I can't say I was. I had an appointment soon with my dentist, not to mention getting my hair cut, the car washed, doing the laundry, grocery-shopping, and all the other things I had yet to deal with that had piled up on my desk while I was away.

"Adam," I called, "I don't have all the time in the world."

He sauntered back. "Forgive me. Without Norman I do tend to dawdle. Now, where were we?"

"Complexes," I said.

Adam settled on a cushion.

"Let us go back to basics," he said. "A complex is an agglomeration of associations, sometimes of traumatic character, sometimes simply painful and highly toned. Anything highly toned is hard to handle. For instance, you may have observed that when you ask me difficult questions I don't answer them immediately. That's because I can't; the subject is important to me and I have a long reaction time. I hesitate; I play for time because my memory doesn't immediately supply the necessary material. We know from Jung's word association experiments what that means, don't we?[74] Such disturbances have their source in complexes.

"Whatever has an intense feeling-tone is difficult to handle because it is associated with physiological reactions—processes of the heart, the tonus of the blood vessels, the condition of the intestines, the breathing, innervation of the skin and so on. It is just as if that particular complex were localized in my body. That makes it unwieldy, because something that irritates my body cannot easily be pushed away; it pulls at my nerves. Something that has little emotional value can be brushed aside because it has no physical roots. It does not adhere."

I wrote this down because some of what Adam was saying I knew but had forgotten, or at least never heard in this way.

"A complex has energy and a life of its own," said Adam. "We might even say it has its own physiology. It can upset the stomach, the breathing, the heart. In short, it behaves like a partial personality. When you want to say or do something and a complex interferes, you find yourself saying or doing something quite different from what you intended. You are simply interrupted. Your best intentions get upset by the complex, exactly as if you had been interfered with by another human being. Thus we are obliged to speak of the tendencies of complexes to act as if they had a certain amount of will power."

Rachel said, "When I took a course in cognitive psychology we were taught that will power was a prerogative of the ego."

"Nominally, it is," replied Adam. "But the ego too is a collection of highly-toned contents, so that in principle there is no difference between it and any other complex. True, the ego is the central complex of consciousness, but when it is swamped by another its will is usurped. Will power, then, is simply a function of the complex that happens to be in

---

[74] See "The Association Method" and "Psychoanalysis and Association Experiments," *Experimental Researches,* CW 2.

charge. Naturally the cognitive school says nothing of this; it is concerned with mental processes, ideas and conscious knowledge, not with the problematic question of where all that comes from."

Rachel made some notes of her own.

Adam said: "Do you remember what Jung said about people having a bee in their bonnet?"[75]

"Meaning an obsessive thought?" I asked.

Adam nodded. "Because complexes have a certain will power, we find that in some conditions, schizophrenia for example, they emancipate themselves from conscious control to such an extent that they can become visible and audible. They appear as visions and speak in voices that are like those of definite people."

I said: "So I'm schizoid, is that what you're saying?"

Adam shrugged. "I am not judging you. The personification of complexes is not in itself pathological. Complexes are regularly personified in dreams, and one can train oneself so they become visible or audible also in a waking condition. It is even psychologically healthy to do so, for when you give them a voice, a face, a personality, they are less likely to take over when you're not looking."

"Is there no such thing as unity of consciousness?" asked Rachel.

"Unity of consciousness," said Adam, "is a wish-dream. We like to think we are one, masters in our own house, but we are not. Even to call it 'our' house is going too far. We are renters at best. Psychologically we live in a boarding house of saints and knaves, nobles and villains, run by a landlord who for all we know is indifferent to the lot. We fancy we can do what we want, but when it comes to a show-down we find that our will is hampered by fellow boarders with a mind of their own.

"Complexes are autonomous groups of associations that have a tendency to move by themselves, to live their own lives in spite of our intentions. Both our personal unconscious and the collective unconscious consist of an unknown number of these fragmentary personalities. This actually explains a lot that is otherwise quite puzzling, like the fact that one has the capacity to dramatize mental contents. When someone creates a

---

[75] See above, p. 59.

character on the stage, or in a poem or novel, do you think it is merely a product of that person's imagination? I think not. That character in a certain way has made itself. A writer may deny that his work has a psychological meaning, but we know differently, don't we?"

Adam looked at me.

"For instance," he said, "you might think you put words into Sunny's mouth, but to my mind you only wrote them down. That was *her* speaking, albeit in yourself. You can read a writer's mind when you study the characters he creates. When I was working with von Franz she told me of a man who after two years of bringing his dreams for analysis confessed that he'd made them all up. 'The joke's on you,' she said. 'Where do you think they came from? You said what was in you. That's as real as any dream.' I myself have worked with writers whose analysis consisted almost entirely of analyzing not their own dreams and behavior but those of their fictional creations. By their lights you shall know them."

I stood up. "And by the time, I'm afraid, I must go. My dentist charges by the minute."

"Must you?" said Adam. "A pity. And Miss Rachel?"

"I'm free for a while," she beamed.

I kissed her. "Take notes," I whispered.

She did, and the following is mostly hers. I say mostly because I compulsively edit everything.

*

I asked Adam: "Do complexes have a consciousness of their own?"

"It is possible," he said. "When we speak of the ego-complex, we naturally assume it has a consciousness, because the relationship of the various contents to the center, in other words to the ego, is called consciousness. But there is also a grouping of contents about a center, a sort of nucleus, in other complexes. What shall we call that, if not consciousness? Have you by any chance ever been to a spiritualist or a seance?"

I shook my head. You know me, I'm as down to earth as . . . well, turnips. (Sorry, couldn't resist.)

"I have," said Adam, "and I was thoroughly convinced that the so-called spirits that manifested through the voice or automatic writing of a medium did indeed have a sort of consciousness of their own. Of course the naive believed the spirits to be the ghosts of a deceased aunt or grand-father or whatever, on account of the more or less distinct personalities that emanated from these manifestations, but I tagged them right away as projected complexes of the medium. So did Jung from his similar experiences; as a young man he wrote a fascinating thesis on it."[76]

We chatted then about what I was up to these days—he's quite knowledgeable about art, you know, and he adores J.K.—until I asked, "So, what do you think really happened to D.?"

"Well," said Adam, "first off, not to put too fine a point on it, he did get into the sauce. As well, he was in a disturbed state of mind, and I think rather more depressed than he realized. Thirdly, he was out of his usual element. As he noted himself, such conditions contribute to a lowering of the level of consciousness, a state in which the inferior function is liable to manifest."

"You suggested he was sidetracked by a complex."

"Yes," said Adam, "in a manner of speaking. You see, the inferior function too is comprised of feeling-toned contents, and that, as I've said, is the basic characteristic of any complex.

"According to Jung's model of typology, three of the four orienting functions may with some application be differentiated, and thus made available to consciousness. A rational type with well-differentiated thinking, for instance, may have at his disposable one, and sometimes two, auxiliary functions of an irrational nature, namely sensation and intuition. But his inferior function, feeling, is bound to be somewhat retarded and contaminated with the unconscious. Of course it wouldn't be completely absent—all the functions are available to each of us to some extent—but tell me now, haven't you noticed that D.'s feeling often goes wildly off on its own?"

"Well . . .," I stalled, not wanting to give away family secrets, "he's reliable, but not entirely predictable."

Adam picked up a book. "Here's what Jung says":

If [the inferior] function, which is still bound indissolubly to the past and whose roots reach back as far as the animal kingdom, can be left behind

---

[76] "On the Psychology and Pathology of So-Called Occult Phenomena," *Psychiatric Studies*, CW 1.

and even forgotten, then consciousness has won for itself a new and not entirely illusory freedom. It can leap over abysses on winged feet; it can free itself from bondage to sense-impressions, emotions, fascinating thoughts, and presentiments by soaring into abstraction. Certain primitive initiations stress the idea of transformation into ghosts and invisible spirits and thereby testify to the relative emancipation of consciousness from the fetters of non-differentiation.[77]

"However," said Adam, "the inferior function too is part of the personality, and when it is left undifferentiated it lapses into unconsciousness and builds up as an element of the shadow. Even when relatively conscious it is autonomous and obsessive; it has the all-or-nothing character of an instinct. Although emancipation from the instincts brings a differentiation and enhancement of consciousness, it can only come about at the expense of the unconscious function, so that conscious orientation lacks what the inferior function could have supplied. Thus, says Jung, 'it often happens that people who have an amazing range of consciousness know less about themselves than the veriest infant.' "[78]

I won't pretend I could follow all this, but at least I understood him to mean that your "gap"—the question you put to Sunny—is feeling. I'm not so sure about that. My experience of you is that your gap, if that's what you want to call it, is more likely intuition—the possibilities, what comes next. I mean, that's why you miss Arnold, isn't it? I don't know; maybe you, we all, have different gaps at different times. And maybe our gaps aren't necessarily typological but something else entirely. It does become complicated, doesn't it?

"The psyche is an intricate interplay of many factors," said Adam. "Typology is only one aspect. The contents of the unconscious consist not only of things that once were conscious but have been repressed, but a good deal that has never been conscious—our potentialities, our unlived life. In Jung's model all that is part and parcel of the shadow. When the time is ripe these unconscious contents will make their presence known and demand to be acknowledged.

---

[77] "A Psychological Approach to the Dogma of the Trinity," *Psychology and Religion,* CW 11, par. 245.
[78] Ibid.

"Now, the behavior of entirely new contents that have been constellated in the unconscious but haven't yet been assimilated to consciousness is similar to that of complexes. They may be based on subliminal perceptions, or they may be creative in character. Like complexes, they lead a life of their own. In the area of artistic and religious phenomena, they commonly appear in personified form—for instance, as noted in D.'s material, as dwarfs or talking animals."

I teased: "Are you and Sunny, then, simply complexes of his?"

Adam smiled. "No more and no less, dear lady, than you are—or than he is one of ours."

Touché, I guess. But did I ever tell you that when he addresses me as "dear lady" I get goose-bumps all over? It just makes me feel so, well, cozy. What complex is that, do you think?

I took a tray of dishes to the sink and when I got back Adam had another book out.

He said: "Here's where Jung talks about the consequences of the psyche's inherent tendency to split":

> [It] means on the one hand dissociation into multiple structural units, but on the other hand the possibility of change and differentiation. It allows certain parts of the psychic structure to be singled out so that, by concentration of the will, they can be trained and brought to their maximum development. In this way certain capacities, especially those that promise to be socially useful, can be fostered to the neglect of others. This produces an unbalanced state similar to that caused by a dominant complex—a change of personality.[79]

"Of course," said Adam, "we don't usually refer to this as obsession by a complex, but as one-sidedness. It is the natural result of concentrating on our best function, which we automatically do because it brings rewards. Still, the end result is much the same as a complex, the only difference being that the one-sidedness is intended and is fostered by every means, whereas a complex, as generally understood, is experienced as an unpleasant disturbance."

He read more:

---

[79] "Psychological Factors in Human Behaviour," *The Structure and Dynamics of the Psyche,* CW 8, par. 255.

People often fail to see that consciously willed one-sidedness is one of the most important causes of an undesirable complex, and that, conversely, certain complexes cause a one-sided differentiation of doubtful value. Some degree of one-sidedness is unavoidable, and, in the same measure, complexes are unavoidable too.[80]

"Looked at in this light, says Jung, complexes might be compared to modified instincts. Listen":

An instinct which has undergone too much psychization can take its revenge in the form of an autonomous complex. This is one of the chief causes of neurosis.[81]

"Psychization?" I asked.

"That's the term Jung used to refer to the process of reflection," explained Adam, "whereby an instinct, or any other unconscious content, is made conscious. Careful observation of oneself is necessary to become conscious, but you can go too far."

Remembering what you wrote—or maybe it was Jung—I said, "Too much civilization makes sick animals?"

"Yes. As I said to D. a few weeks ago in Mayday's, chaff has its place. Come to think of it, even wheat can become a complex."

Remind me to ask you about that. I think it must be important because Adam *chortled.* Isn't that a good word to describe the way he laughs? It's just that little bit sinister.

"To my mind," said Adam, "that is the why and wherefore of D.'s active imagination. In any exercise of that sort, the danger is that the ego cannot withstand the weight of the unconscious contents that manifest. Instead of relating to the Self, the ego dissolves in identification with it. The result is a sort of nebulous superman with an inflated ego—D. as the Philosophers' Stone!—and a deflated Self. He made a brave sortie into never-never land and ran aground. Better luck next time."

I looked at my watch; I'd promised J.K. I'd meet her after school to go for tattoos.

"Tell me," I said, "why is it so necessary to bring unconscious con-

---

[80] Ibid.
[81] Ibid.

tents up? If the psyche is self-regulating, don't they come up by themselves? And didn't all the important stuff come out in D.'s analysis?"

"They are good questions," said Adam. "Unfortunately, analysis is not a once-and-for-all cure. It is only a more or less thorough readjustment of the psychological attitude to one better suited to current inner and outer conditions. The new attitude may last a long time, but there is no change that is unconditionally or permanently valid. The flow of life continually presents us with problematic situations requiring fresh adaptation.

"Directedness is necessary for the conscious process, but as I pointed out earlier it entails an unavoidable one-sidedness. So consciousness easily overlooks or suppresses compensating influences, which then accumulate in the unconscious. Here is how Jung put it":

> Were it not for the directedness of the conscious attitude, the counteracting influences of the unconscious could set in unhindered. It is just this directedness that excludes them. This, of course, does not inhibit the counteraction, which goes on in spite of everything. Its regulating influence, however, is eliminated by critical attention and the directed will, because the counteraction as such seems incompatible with the conscious direction. To this extent the psyche of civilized man is no longer a self-regulating system but could rather be compared to a machine whose speed-regulation is so insensitive that it can continue to function to the point of self-injury.[82]

"You see," said Adam, "it is a peculiarity of psychic functioning that when the unconscious counteraction is suppressed it loses its regulating influence. Jung says":

> A condition then arises in which not only no inhibiting counteraction takes place, but in which its energy seems to add itself to that of the conscious direction. To begin with, this naturally facilitates the execution of the conscious intentions, but because they are unchecked, they may easily assert themselves at the cost of the whole. For instance, when someone makes a rather bold assertion and suppresses a well-placed doubt, he will insist on it all the more, to his own detriment.[83]

"The participation of the unconscious in our lives is everywhere present, but as long as it remains unconscious we never really know what is going on or what to expect. How are we to find out? Without a natural

---

[82] "The Transcendent Function," ibid., par. 159.
[83] Ibid.

capacity to produce fantasies, we are obliged to resort to artificial aids. Active imagination is the method Jung developed to make conscious psychic contents that are about to influence us. He saw this as the beginning of the transcendent function—the collaboration of conscious and unconscious, ego and Self—but of course that's a topic in itself."

I gathered my things. "Dear Adam, I could listen to you forever, but I really have to go."

We hugged.

"Wouldn't you care for a nap first?" said Adam. "There's the honeymoon suite . . ."

I smiled.

"Well," he said, "you might just think of this. Did D. discover what was needful?"

"You'll have to put that to him," I said.

I was halfway out the door when Adam said, "Oh Miss Rachel, by the way . . . did he really go to Manitoulin?"

It was like that TV program we watch, *Columbo;* just when the bad guy thinks he's safe, Detective Columbo nails him to the wall. You wonder: how did he know?

"He needed a break," said Adam. "I suggested he use my cottage. I gave him a key. But did he go?"

I looked at him. "Ibsen wrote about Norway from a desk in Italy. James Joyce described Dublin from a Paris garret. Willa Cather wrote prairie novels from an apartment in New York City. Walt Whitman rarely left his room. Do you think Jules Verne went 20,000 leagues under the sea? Myself, I paint landscapes in my studio. And you, Adam, were you really ever in the Himalayas? Borneo?"

He had the grace to blush.

*

"Excellent work," I said. "I think I'll use it."

"Thank you," said Rachel.

We were having breakfast in her kitchen, a rare occurrence. Usually when I stay over at her place I am up and gone by six, after loving her, one way or another, and pecking J.K.'s sleeping cheek. This morning I had unaccountably slept in.

"So," I said, tapping my knee, "I'm reliable but not entirely predictable. What's that supposed to mean?"

Rachel was making herself a frothy capuccino on her new machine. She'd already made me one.

"It bothered you?" she said.

I looked away.

"Dummy. It means I trust you, even though you don't always do what I expect. It's a compliment, really. Our relationship is not routine. There's always something new."

"And trust?" I asked.

"You won't let me down," she said.

This was about as close to working on our relationship as Rachel and I ever get. Not that there's much to work on, but when we realize we've touched a complex we try to tiptoe around it.

"You didn't notice my tattoo," she said. She raised her skirt to show me. On her ankle was the outline of two fishes, head to head, a heart in between. Rachel is a Pisces: two fishes, the opposites, under her skin and now on it.

"That's you and me," she said, "among other things. And glad of it."

I hugged her. "Love you."

"I do love you too."

11
Stages of Life

"The wine of youth does not always clear with advancing years," said Adam. "Sometimes it grows turbid."

We were back in Mayday Malone's, enjoying a quiet pint. It was two o'clock on a Thursday afternoon in February. Adam and I were among the very few patrons. Sunny snoozed at my feet. The TV sets were off; no one was playing games.

"Statistics show a rise in the frequency of depression in men at the age of about forty," said Adam, "in women somewhat earlier. In this phase of life, between thirty-five and forty, an important change in the psyche is in preparation. At first it is not conscious or striking, simply indirect signs of a change which seems to take its rise in the unconscious. Often it manifests as a slow change in a person's character; in other cases certain traits may come to light which had been dormant since childhood; or again, one's previous inclinations and interests begin to weaken and others take their place. Conversely, one's cherished convictions and principles, especially moral ones, begin to harden and grow increasingly rigid.

"All this can best be seen in rather one-sided people, occurring sometimes sooner and sometimes later. Often their appearance is delayed by the fact that the parents of the person are still alive. It is then as if the period of youth were being unduly drawn out. I have noticed this especially in the case of men whose fathers were long-lived. The death of the father then has the effect of a precipitate and almost catastrophic ripening."

"My father was alive when I ripened," I said. "I was thirty-seven years old. I woke up crying one morning and couldn't stop. I was a basket case. It was the end of life as I knew it."

"Yes, I remember," said Adam. "You were lucky; you had time left."

We sipped our beer.

"The psychic life of civilized man is full of problems," Adam said. "We can hardly think of it except in terms of problems. Our psychic processes are made up to a large extent of reflections, doubts and experiments that are almost completely foreign to the unconscious, instinctive mind of primitive man. As long as we live submerged in nature we are unconscious; we live in the security of instinct which knows no problems. Everything in us that still belongs to nature shrinks away from a problem, for its name is doubt, and wherever doubt holds sway there is uncertainty, the possibility of divergent ways. And where several ways seem possible, we have lost the guidance of instinct and are in the clutches of fear—fear of being wrong, of not making the right decision."

"But don't our very problems bring the possibility of a widening of consciousness?"

"Indeed," said Adam, "but they also require us to say good-bye to a childlike unconsciousness and trust in nature. This necessity is a psychic fact so important that it constitutes one of the most essential symbolic teachings of Christianity. It is the sacrifice of the merely natural man, of the unconscious, ingenuous being whose tragic career began with the eating of the apple in Paradise. The Biblical fall of man presents the dawn of consciousness as a curse. And in fact it is in this light that we first experience every problem that forces us to greater consciousness and separates us even further from the paradise of unconscious childhood.

"Think how we turn away from our problems. If possible they must not be mentioned; better still, their existence is denied. We wish our lives to be simple and smooth, and for that reason problems are taboo. We want certainties and no doubts—results and no experiments—without realizing that certainties can arise only through doubt, and results only through experiment. The artful denial of a problem does not produce conviction."

"Back to nature, then, is it?" I joshed.

Adam laughed.

"Do you remember what Jung said?" He looked off. "Something like: 'There is nothing to stop you from taking a two-room cottage in the country, or from puttering about in a garden and eating raw turnips. But your soul will laugh at the deception.'[84]

"No, I'm afraid we're stuck with consciousness as a way out. A wider and higher consciousness is required to give us the certainty and clarity

---

[84] Adam was close enough; see *Two Essays,* par. 258.

we need. When we have a problem, we instinctively resist trying the way out that leads through obscurity and darkness. But in order to penetrate the darkness we must summon all the powers of enlightenment that consciousness can offer. We must even indulge in speculation. In treating the problems of psychic life, for instance, we continually stumble upon questions of principle belonging to diverse branches of knowledge. We disturb and anger the theologian no less than the philosopher, the physician no less than the educator; we even grope about in the domains of the biologist and the historian.

"This is not arrogance but due to the fact that the psyche is a unique combination of factors which at one and the same time are the special subjects of far-reaching lines of research. Out of himself and his peculiar constitution man has produced the sciences. They are symptoms of the human psyche."

The waiter intruded. "You guys okay here?"

We ordered another round.

"Where's Winona?" I asked Adam.

"She left last week. They say she went to live in the woods with a hunter." He chuckled. "And good luck to them."

"Adam," I said, "why do we have problems at all, and apparently other animals don't?"

He hunched forward.

"We can thank the growth of consciousness for the existence of problems," he said. "There are no problems without consciousness. We should therefore ask, rather, how consciousness arises in the first place.

"Now, no one knows for certain, but we can watch small children in the process of becoming conscious. When the child recognizes someone or something, then we feel it has consciousness. At this level, consciousness is limited to the perception of a few connections between psychic contents. There is no continuous memory in the early years of life; at most there are islands of consciousness, like single lamps or lighted objects in the dark. Gradually the contents of these islands are recognized as belonging to the perceiving subject, the so-called ego. The feeling of 'I-ness' arises; the child begins to speak of itself in the first person.

"In the childish stage of consciousness there are as yet no problems;

nothing depends upon the subject, for the child is still wholly dependent on its parents. It is as though it were not yet completely born, but still enclosed in the psychic atmosphere of the parents. Of course the complex psychic life of the child is a significant problem to parents, educators and doctors, but the normal child has no real problems of its own. Only the adult human being can have self-doubts, the sine qua non of problems.

"Take yourself. You wrote about being answerable to no one, yes?"

I nodded.

"And yet, when you have time to think, or just out of the blue, you are troubled by questions, is that true?"

"It is," I said.

"That is the price we pay," said Adam, "for being grown up."

I'd never thought of it like that.

"Individual psychic birth," said Adam, "and with it conscious differentiation from the parents, usually takes place only at puberty, with the eruption of sexuality. Until then psychic life is governed largely by instinct and few or no problems arise. Even when external limitations oppose subjective impulses, we submit to them or circumvent them; one is not at variance with oneself, does not yet know the state of inner tension induced by a problem. This state only arises when what was an external limitation becomes an inner one—when one impulse is opposed by another with equal intensity. Then we have self-division, the dualistic state characteristic of problems and conflicts in the period of youth."

"How long does that last?" I asked. Of course I should have known. I'd read Jung's essay, "The Stages of Life,"[85] but that was years ago. One reason I valued my time with Adam was that he remembered so much I had forgotten.

"Most developmentalists," said Adam, "consider youth to extend for twenty years or so, from just after puberty to middle life, say thirty-five or forty. Many sources of problems in this period are due to the clash between reality and illusions or false assumptions: exaggerated expectations, underestimating difficulties, unjustified optimism, a negative attitude and so on. But just as often it is inner, psychic difficulties that give

---

[85] *The Structure and Dynamics of the Psyche,* CW 8.

rise to problems, even when adaptation to the outer world has been achieved without apparent effort. Indeed, it sometimes seems as if those who have had a hard struggle for existence are spared inner problems, while those who have experienced no difficulty at all in adaptation have sexual problems or conflicts arising from a sense of inferiority."

"Do you think some people are temperamentally neurotic?" I asked.

Adam shrugged.

"Those who have problems due to their own temperaments are often neurotic. But let us not confuse the existence of problems with neurosis. The neurotic suffers because he is unconscious of his problems. A person with a difficult temperament may suffer from conscious problems without being neurotic.

"In the myriad variety of individual problems found in the period of youth, there is invariably one common factor: a resistance to growing up. Something in us wishes to remain a child, to stay unconscious; to reject everything strange, or else subject it to our will; to do nothing, or else indulge our craving for pleasure or power. In all this there is something of the inertia of matter, a persistence in the childish stage of consciousness that is narrower and more egoistic than the dualistic phase, which offers a widening of the horizon of life. But it is just this that is so vigorously resisted. To be sure, this expansion begins at birth, when the child abandons the narrow confines of the mother's body. From then on it steadily increases until it reaches a climax in the problematical state, at which point one begins to struggle against it.

"Psychology teaches us that there is nothing in the psyche that is old; nothing that can really, finally, die away. Even St. Paul was left with a thorn in the flesh. Whoever protects himself against what is new and strange and regresses to the past falls into the same neurotic condition as the one who identifies with the new and runs away from the past. The only difference is that the one has estranged himself from the past and the other from the future. In principle both are doing the same thing: reinforcing their narrow range of consciousness instead of shattering it in the tension of opposites that leads to wider and deeper consciousness."

"Most people," I observed, "strive to achieve or to be useful. Is that not enough?"

"Enough? I don't know," said Adam. "Clearly many think it is. I once did myself. Now I find such pursuits superficial. But there's the rub. Society does not value consciousness of oneself; its prizes are not given for personality except, sometimes, posthumously.

"Consciousness can only seek culture or its denial. Achievement, usefulness and so forth are the ideals that seem to point the way out of the confusions of the problematical state. They are the lodestars that guide us in the adventure of broadening and consolidating our physical existence; they help us strike our roots in the world. In the youthful years this course is the usual one, and certainly preferable to flailing about in a welter of problems. But it does little to develop that wider consciousness to which we give the name of culture.

"The dilemmas we meet in the period of youth are generally dealt with by adapting whatever was given to us by the past to the possibilities and demands of the future. We limit ourselves to the attainable, and this means renouncing all our other psychic potentialities. One person loses a valuable piece of the past, another a valuable piece of the future. Think of those you went to school with and looked up to, promising young minds destined for greatness, and when you met them years later they seemed dry and cramped, stuck in a narrow mold."

Several came to my mind. But I wondered: if the same question were put to them, might I come to theirs? To others, Jungian psychology might well seem to be a narrow mold, or even, as some have suggested, a moldy cult. What's in a mold? Was I in one?

I had no heart to put these questions to Adam. He was on a roll. I listened as he pursued the bee in his bonnet.

"The serious problems in life," said Adam, "are never completely solved. If ever they should appear to be, it is a sure sign that something has been lost. The meaning and purpose of a problem seem to lie not in its solution but in our working at it incessantly."

"Something like Sunny worrying a bone?" I asked. She stirred at her name; I patted her and slipped her a cookie—uncomfortably aware that I was throwing yet another sop, so to speak, to Cerberus, the fearsome hound who guards the gateway to the Underworld.

"A fair analogy," said Adam. "As a solution to the problems of youth, restricting ourselves to the attainable works only temporarily; it is not lasting in a deeper sense. Of course, to win for oneself a place in society and to transform one's nature so that it is more or less fitted to this kind of existence is no small achievement. It involves a fight within oneself as well as outside, comparable to the struggle of the child for an ego. That struggle for the most part goes on unobserved because it happens in the dark. But when we see how stubbornly childish illusions and assumptions are still clung to in later years, we can gain some idea of the energies that were needed to form them. And so it is with the ideals, convictions, guiding ideas and attitudes that in the period of youth lead us out into life, for which we struggle, suffer and win victories. In a certain way we become them and seek to perpetuate them indefinitely.

"The closer we come to midlife, and the better we have succeeded in entrenching ourselves in our personal attitudes and social positions, the more it seems as if we had discovered the right course, the right ideals and principles of behavior. Thus we suppose them to be eternally valid and even make a virtue of clinging to them, overlooking the fact that social goals are by and large attained at the cost of a diminution of personality. Aspects of life which should also have been experienced gather dust in the wood shed, or are faintly glowing coals under gray ashes.

"Around the age of fifty, a period of intolerance and fanaticism is reached. It is as if the existence of one's principles were endangered and it were therefore necessary to emphasize them all the more. This is another peak time for neurotic disturbances, which now have in common the desire to carry the psychology of youth over the threshold of the so-called years of discretion. Who does not know those touching old folk who must forever warm up the dish of their past, who can fan the flame of life only by recalling their heroic youth, stuck in a kind of hopeless Philistinism?"

I knew some. "Are they necessarily neurotic?" I asked.

"Not so's you'd notice," said Adam, "only boring and stereotyped. I would reserve the term neurotic for those who can never have things as they would like them in the present, and who can therefore never enjoy the past either.

"As formerly the neurotic resisted the move out of childhood, so now he cannot part from youth. He is consumed by gray thoughts of approaching age and is always straining to look behind. Just as the childish person shrinks back from the unknown in the world, the challenge of uncertainty, so the grown-up shrinks back from the second half of life. It is as if unknown and dangerous tasks awaited, or as if they were threatened with unacceptable sacrifices and losses—as if life up to now were so fair and precious it could not be relinquished."

"Is it the fear of death, do you think?"

Adam shook his head. "I doubt it. I felt those tremors myself thirty-odd years ago, when death was a lot further in the future than it is now. In the meantime I have adjusted and feel nothing of the sort, but that's another story. No, the basic difficulty in the transition from middle life to old age seems to be due to a deep-seated change within the psyche. Jung characterized this change by comparing it to the daily course of the sun—but a sun endowed with human feeling and our limited consciousness."

He looked at me slyly and pulled a scrap of paper from his pocket. "I wrote it down so I wouldn't forget." And he read:

> In the morning [the sun] rises from the nocturnal sea of unconsciousness and looks upon the wide, bright world which lies before it in an expanse that steadily widens the higher it climbs in the firmament. In this extension of its field of action caused by its own rising, the sun will discover its significance; it will see the attainment of the greatest possible height, and the widest possible dissemination of its blessings, as its goal. In this conviction the sun pursues its course to the unforeseen zenith—unforeseen, because its career is unique and individual, and the culminating point could not be calculated in advance. At the stroke of noon the descent begins. And the descent means the reversal of all the ideals and values that were cherished in the morning. The sun falls into contradiction with itself. It is as though it should draw in its rays instead of emitting them. Light and warmth decline and are at last extinguished.[86]

"Very poetic," I said, "but I don't feel like a setting sun."

Adam harumphed.

"Do you think anyone your age does? Even I, considerably closer to the nadir, don't. Whole industries and billions of dollars are devoted to

---

[86] Ibid., par. 778.

telling us we are still on the rise. That doesn't change the fact that we aren't. I agree with Jung that there is something sunlike within us. To speak of the morning and the spring, of the evening and autumn of life, is not merely sentimental jargon. These are psychological truths. More, they express physiological facts, for the reversal of the sun at noon changes even bodily characteristics. Older women often develop deep or rough voices and incipient mustaches, rather hard features and other traits traditionally seen as masculine. The masculine physique is toned down by feminine features—adiposity and softer facial expressions.

"Jung tells of an Indian warrior chief to whom in middle life the Great Spirit appeared in a dream. The spirit told him that from then on he must sit with the women and children, wear women's clothes, eat the food of women and do the work of women. He obeyed and suffered no loss of prestige. His vision was understood by all to be a true expression of the psychic revolution of life's noon, of the beginning of life's decline. Our values, and our bodies, do tend to change into their opposites."

"I'm not an Indian, either," I said.

Adam sat back. "A bit cranky, are we? Well, suit yourself."

He scoured the bowl of his pipe and set about refilling it.

I grimaced. Again, I was suddenly, and unaccountably, contentious. I flipped through my internal inventory and there was Arnold, leering, wagging his finger. Don't believe anything you hear and only half of what you read, he admonished. Get lost, I said, I will decide for myself. Arnold vanished.

"Sorry, Adam, you were saying?"

He continued: "Think of masculinity and femininity and their psychic components as a definite store of substances of which unequal use is made by either sex in the first half of life. A man consumes his large supply of masculine substance and has left over an amount of feminine substance which must now be put to use. Similarly, a women runs dry of her own stuff and finds a hitherto unused supply of masculinity at her disposal."

He eyed me. "Okay so far?"

I nodded. There is some dispute these days over what is masculine and what is feminine, but I can live, as Jung did, with the *consensus gen-*

tium—what people have always and ever believed. However vague or to some minds sexist, the terms masculine and feminine are still relevant psychologically, as two complementary energies.

"The psychic change at midlife is even more noticeable," said Adam. "How often it happens that a man of forty-five or fifty winds down his business, and the wife then opens a little shop and he takes on the duties of a handyman. Many women only awaken to social consciousness and responsibility after they're forty. In fact the forties are also the years when nervous breakdowns are common among men in business life. It is as if what has broken down is the masculine style of striving that brought him everything he has, and what is left over is an ineffectual, even effeminate, man. Likewise, women in the second half of life often develop a masculine tough-mindedness that puts the heart in second place."

"And what that does to a relationship!" I blurted out.

"It can be catastrophic," agreed Adam, "when the man discovers his tender feelings and the women her sharpness of mind."

"It is a shame we aren't taught about the possibility of such transformations," I said. "Perhaps someone, some day, will start a school for forty-year-olds to prepare them for later life and its demands—like colleges and universities introduce young people to a knowledge of the world."

"Religions were such schools in the past," said Adam. "They prepared the faithful for old age, death and eternity. They still do, of course, but few are there to listen. Now most of us take the step into the afternoon of life wholly innocent of what to expect; worse, we take this step believing that our truths and ideals will serve us as before. We imagine we can live the afternoon of life according to the morning's program. We are shocked to discover this fundamental truth: that what in the morning was true, in the evening is a lie."

I said: "What if more people went into analysis? Maybe, in this day and age, that would be the best preparation for later life."

Adam mused.

"I would like to think that analysis is the answer," he said. "It was for me; it worked for you and for many we know. But in my heart of hearts I believe that analysis doesn't take until and unless you've hit a brick wall in your life. As well, I know that many are not suited to the rigorous process of coming to terms with the unconscious. Few have the mind or time for it; friends and relatives scoff. It can be a very lonely journey."

He lowered his head. Of a sudden I realized I knew next to nothing of Adam's personal life, his relationships, his sacrifices along the way. His ideas were an open book; the rest he kept pretty much to himself.

"Aging people," he said, "should know that their lives are not mounting and expanding, but that an inexorable inner process enforces the contraction of energy. When you're young it is almost a sin to be too preoccupied with yourself, but for the elderly it is a duty and a necessity to devote serious attention to the inner life. Having lavished its light upon the world, the sun withdraws its rays in order to illuminate itself. Instead of doing the same, many old people choose to be hypochondriacs, whining niggards, stingy pedants or else eternal adolescents—puers at sixty!—all lamentable substitutes for self-knowledge, but inevitable consequences of the delusion that the second half of life can be governed by the principles that sufficed in the first. Longevity must have a meaning for us. Why else would nature allow us to live to seventy, eighty, ninety and more? Is the afternoon of life merely a pitiful appendage to life's morning?"

Adam was quite steamed. I liked to see him this way: heartily decrying the failings of those in his own age group while personally belying them.

"I think not," he said. "The significance of the morning undoubtedly lies in the development of our individual talents and abilities, entrenchment in the outer world, the propagation and care of offspring. All of nature supports and speaks to this. But what then? When this purpose has been attained and fulfilled? Shall the earning of money, the extension of conquests, the building of status, go steadily on and on, beyond the bounds of all reason and sense? Halt! I say. Look at yourself."

Now this hit home. In terms of age and position, I was over the hill. Maybe it was time I stopped climbing. But say I did, what would I do instead? And how would my shadow react?

"Whoever carries over into the afternoon of life the law of the morning," said Adam, "must pay for it with damage to his soul, just as surely as the growing youth who carries childish egoism into adult life must pay for his mistake with social failure. Money making, social achievement, family and posterity, these are all plain nature, not culture. Culture lies outside the purpose of nature."

I said, "So, do you think culture could be the meaning and purpose of the second half of life?"

"It is possible," he nodded. "In primitive tribes old people are the guardians of the mysteries and the laws, and it is in these that the cultural heritage of the tribe is expressed. In our own society, where is the hard-won wisdom of our old people? Where are their precious secrets and their visions?" He fumed. "For the most part, our old people try to compete with the young; the ideal is for the father to be the brother of his sons, while the mother does her best to be the younger sister of her daughter."

"In olden times," I said, "age had dignity."

"Please," said Adam, "spare me that. I suspect that the dignity traditionally accorded to old people was deserved by only a few. In that respect, nothing has changed. When my own day is done, I would much rather be set adrift on an ice-floe with a biscuit—a double Oreo, please, if you have a say—as was the Inuit custom, than be honored simply because I'm old."

"What about immortality?" I asked. "Life after death?"

Adam took a deep swig of beer. He spread his hands.

"Concerning such questions there are innumerable contradictory opinions and no convincing proofs, no definite scientific knowledge one way or the other about what does or does not happen to a person after death. We are in the same position as when we ask if the planet Mars is inhabited or not. And the inhabitants of Mars, if there are any, are certainly not concerned one way or the other with what we think. They may exist or they may not. That is how it stands with so-called immortality.

"However, I have observed that a life directed toward an aim is in general better, richer and healthier than an aimless one, and that it is wiser to go forward with the stream of time than backward against the current. An old person who cannot bid farewell to life is little different from a young one who is unable to embrace it. And in fact it is often a question of the self-same childish greediness, the same fear, the same defiance and willfulness, in the one as in the other.

"On the whole, I believe that it is psychologically healthy to discover in death a goal toward which one can gladly move, and that shrinking away from it is what robs the second half of life of its purpose. Although I long ago stopped going to any church, I do believe that religions with a supramundane goal are eminently reasonable from the point of view of psychic health. Thus it is desirable to think of death as only a transition, as part of a life process whose extent and duration are beyond our knowing. Indeed, by far the greater part of mankind has from time immemorial felt the need to believe in the continuance of life. It is like not knowing why the body needs salt; everyone demands it nonetheless, because of an instinctive need. The ancient *athanasias pharmakon,* the medicine of immortality, is more profound and meaningful than we might think."

I asked: "Do you mean, then, that in spite of all evidence to the contrary, we should carry on as if we would live forever?"

"Why not?" said Adam. "The psyche does. The dreams recorded by dying people are not grim depictions of an impending end; they are little different from before.

"Come back for a moment to the comparison with the sun. The one hundred and eighty degrees of the arc of life are divisible into four parts. The first quarter, to the east, is childhood, that state in which we are a problem for others but are not yet conscious of any problems of our own. Conscious problems fill out the second and third quarters; and in the last, in extreme old age, we descend again into that condition where, regardless of our state of consciousness, we once more become a problem for others. Of course childhood and old age are different, yet they have one thing in common: submersion in unconscious psychic happenings."

I thought about that for a few minutes. Then I asked, "Adam, do you think consciousness can serve us as well as nature?"

"The verdict is not yet in on that," he said. "Jung believed that the reason why consciousness exists, and why there is an urge to widen and deepen it, is very simple: without consciousness things go less well.[87] Unfortunately, the opposite may also be true. Everything depends on how

---

[87] "Analytical Psychology and 'Weltanschauung,' " *The Structure and Dynamics of the Psyche,* CW 8, par. 695.

we use our consciousness. We have conquered the earth, but the triumph over nature easily leads to hubris. By becoming conscious we have usurped powers previously reserved for the gods. Whether in the last analysis this is an advantage or a calamity we are not in a position to know."

We nursed our last drops of beer.

"Where are you with your book?" asked Adam.

"Almost finished."

"Am I in it?"

"You have a cameo or two," I admitted.

Adam leaned forward. "Did you do what you intended? Did you say what you meant?"

I squirmed, thinking of the detours not of my making, dead-ends, un-foreseen complications, the bits and pieces that got out of hand. But there you are: I was at the helm, but my craft was subject to the wind.

"Honestly, Adam, could you, could anyone, answer an unequivocal Yes to such questions?"

He shrugged. He drained his glass and stood up. I did the same. He donned cape and beret and twirled his cane. Jaunty. Sunny came awake and stretched her legs. She knows when a walk is coming, just from the cut of my jib.

Adam hugged her. "There's a good girl."

He turned to me.

"Thank you for the afternoon. Now the evening beckons. Shall we de-bouche to my place? I have some new things that might interest you. Just yesterday I came into possession of a rare alchemical text. Do you agree? Fine! Pick up the tab, would you? There's a good fellow."

I did wish he'd said better.

Bibliography

Bennet, Doug, and Tiner, Tim. *Up North: A Guide to Ontario's Wilderness from Blackflies to the Northern Lights.* Markham, ON: Reed Books, 1993.

Dostoyevsky. Fyodor. *Notes from Underground.* New York: New American Library, 1961.

Frantz, Gilda. "I'll See You in My Dreams." In *Psychological Perspectives,* no. 31 (Spring-Summer 1995).

Johnston, Basil. *Ojibway Heritage: The Ceremonies, Rituals and Legends of the Ojibway.* Toronto: McClelland and Stewart, 1976.

Jung, C.G. *C.G. Jung Speaking: Interviews and Encounters* (Bollingen Series XCVII). Ed. Wm. McGuire, R.F.C. Hull. Princeton: Princeton University Press, 1977.

————. *The Collected Works* (Bollingen Series XX). 20 vols. Trans. R.F.C. Hull. Ed. H. Read, M. Fordham, G. Adler, Wm. McGuire. Princeton: Princeton University Press, 1953-1979.

Kafka, Franz. *The Penal Colony: Stories and Short Pieces.* Trans. Willa and Edwin Muir. New York: Schocken Books, 1961.

Sharp, Daryl. *The Secret Raven: Conflict and Transformation in the Life of Franz Kafka.* Toronto: Inner City Books, 1980.

————. *Personality Types: Jung's Model of Typology.* Toronto: Inner City Books, 1987.

————. *The Survival Papers: Anatomy of a Midlife Crisis.* Toronto: Inner City Books, 1988.

————. *Jung Lexicon: A Primer of Terms and Concepts.* Toronto: Inner City Books, 1991.

————. *Getting To Know You: The Inside Out of Relationship.* Toronto: Inner City Books, 1992.

————. *Chicken Little: The Inside Story (A Jungian Romance).* Toronto: Inner City Books, 1993.

————. *Who Am I, Really? Personality, Soul and Individuation.* Toronto: Inner City Books, 1995.

von Franz, Marie-Louise. *A Psychological Interpretation of the Golden Ass of Apuleius.* Zürich: Spring Publications, 1970.

————. *Puer Aeternus: A Psychological Study of the Adult Struggle with the Paradise of Childhood.* 2nd ed. Santa Monica: Sigo Press, 1981.

Index

OTHER INNER CITY TITLES

The Creation of Consciousness: Jung's Myth for Modern Man
Edward F. Edinger (Los Angeles) ISBN 0-919123-13-9. Illustrated. 128 pp. $15

Conscious Femininity: Interviews with Marion Woodman
Introduction by Marion Woodman (Toronto) ISBN 0-919123-59-7. 160 pp. $16

The Middle Passage: From Misery to Meaning in Midlife
James Hollis (Philadelphia) ISBN 0-919123-60-0. 128 pp. $15

Eros and Pathos: Shades of Love and Suffering
Aldo Carotenuto (Rome) ISBN 0-919123-39-2. 144 pp. $16

Descent to the Goddess: A Way of Initiation for Women
Sylvia Brinton Perera (New York) ISBN 0-919123-05-8. 112 pp. $15

Addiction to Perfection: The Still Unravished Bride
Marion Woodman (Toronto) ISBN 0-919123-11-2. Illustrated. 208 pp. $18

Coming To Age: The Croning Years and Late-Life Transformation
Jane R. Prétat (Providence, RI) ISBN 0-919123-63-5. 144 pp. $16

Jungian Dream Interpretation: A Handbook of Theory and Practice
James A. Hall, M.D. (Dallas) ISBN 0-919123-12-0. 128 pp. $15

Jung Lexicon: A Primer of Terms & Concepts
Daryl Sharp (Toronto) ISBN 0-919123-48-1. Diagrams. 160 pp. $16

The Sacred Prostitute: Eternal Aspect of the Feminine
Nancy Qualls-Corbett (Birmingham) ISBN 0-919123-31-7. Illustrated. 176 pp. $18

The Aion Lectures: Exploring the Self in C.G. Jung's *Aion*
Edward F. Edinger (Los Angeles) ISBN 0-919123-72-4. 30 illustrations. 208 pp. $18

Prices and payment in $US (in Canada, $Cdn)
Discounts: any 3-5 books, 10%; 6 books or more, 20%
Add Postage/Handling: 1-2 books, $2; 3-4 books, $4; 5-9 books, $8
Write or phone for free Catalogue of over 70 titles

INNER CITY BOOKS
Studies in Jungian Psychology by Jungian Analysts
Box 1271, Station Q, Toronto, ON M4T 2P4, Canada   (416) 927-0355

2483